C000145949

1 MONTH OF
FREE
READING

at

www.ForgottenBooks.com

By purchasing this book you are eligible for one month membership to ForgottenBooks.com, giving you unlimited access to our entire collection of over 1,000,000 titles via our web site and mobile apps.

To claim your free month visit:

www.forgottenbooks.com/free1116254

* Offer is valid for 45 days from date of purchase. Terms and conditions apply.

ISBN 978-0-331-38684-4
PIBN 11116254

This book is a reproduction of an important historical work. Forgotten Books uses state-of-the-art technology to digitally reconstruct the work, preserving the original format whilst repairing imperfections present in the aged copy. In rare cases, an imperfection in the original, such as a blemish or missing page, may be replicated in our edition. We do, however, repair the vast majority of imperfections successfully; any imperfections that remain are intentionally left to preserve the state of such historical works.

Forgotten Books is a registered trademark of FB &c Ltd.
Copyright © 2018 FB &c Ltd.
FB &c Ltd, Dalton House, 60 Windsor Avenue, London, SW19 2RR.
Company number 08720141. Registered in England and Wales.

For support please visit www.forgottenbooks.com

Historic, Archive Document

Do not assume content reflects current scientific knowledge, policies, or practices

United States Department of Agriculture

FOOD AND DRUG ADMINISTRATION

NOTICES OF JUDGMENT UNDER THE INSECTICIDE ACT

[Given pursuant to section 4 of the Insecticide Act]

1376–1425

[Approved by the Acting Secretary of Agriculture, Washington, D. C., March 14, 1936]

1376. Misbranding of Star Liquid Lime Sulphurous Compound. U. S. v. William Jesse Lindsey (Star Chemical Co.). Plea of guilty. Fine, $25. (I. & F. no. 1618. Sample no. 16642–A.)

This case was based on an interstate shipment of a product which was an insecticide within the meaning of the law, and which contained inert ingredients that were not declared on the label as required by law.

On July 17, 1934, the United States attorney for the Northern District of Texas, acting upon a report by the Secretary of Agriculture, filed in the district court an information against William Jesse Lindsey, trading as the Star Chemical Co., Arlington, Tex., alleging shipment by said defendant on or about June 20, 1932, from the State of Texas into the State of Georgia of a quantity of Star Liquid Lime Sulphurous Compound which was a misbranded insecticide, other than Paris green and lead arsenate, within the meaning of the Insecticide Act of 1910.

The article was alleged to be misbranded in that it consisted completely of inert substances or ingredients, that is to say, substances that do not prevent, destroy, repel, or mitigate insects when used as directed, and the name and the percentage amount of each of said inert substances present in the article were not stated plainly and correctly on the bottle label. The information also charged a violation of the Food and Drugs Act reported in notice of judgment no. 24122 published under that act.

On December 5, 1934, the defendant entered a plea of guilty and the court imposed a fine of $25 as penalty for violation of both acts.

M. L. WILSON, *Acting Secretary of Agriculture.*

1377. Misbranding of Apex Cresola Disinfectant. U. S. v. Apex Soap & Sanitary Corporation. Plea of guilty. Fine, $50 and costs. (I. & F. no. 1766. Sample no. 60885–A.)

This case was based on an interstate shipment of a product which was misbranded because of unwarranted claims in the labeling regarding its alleged disinfecting, germicidal, and sterilizing properties.

On February 6, 1935, the United States attorney for the Western District of Pennsylvania, acting upon a report by the Secretary of Agriculture, filed in the district court an information against the Apex Soap & Sanitary Corporation, Pittsburgh, Pa., alleging shipment by said company, on or about September 21, 1933, from the State of Pennsylvania into the State of Ohio of a quantity of Apex Cresola Disinfectant, which was a misbranded insecticide and fungicide within the meaning of the Insecticide Act of 1910.

The article was alleged to be misbranded in that the following statements appearing on the can label, "General Disinfection Add three tablespoonful of Apex Cresola to a pail of water used in mopping, scrubbing and cleaning, making sure to place Apex Cresola in the pail first, before adding water; this solution will make a cleaner, deodorant and germicide", "Disinfectant * * * Sinks, drains, urinals, water closets, outdoor vaults—Mix three tablespoonful of Apex Cresola to one gallon of water and stir thoroughly. Flush bowls, pans and vaults morning and night", "Cuspidors—Always use a solution of Disinfectant when cleaning cuspidors. Three tablespoonsful of Apex Cresola to one gallon of water will sterilize and deodorize them and kill bacteria incident to sputum. Leave a solution standing in the cuspidor", were false and misleading, and by reason of the said statements the article was labeled so as to deceive and mislead the purchaser, in that the said statements represented that the article, when used for general disinfection in the dilution of three tablespoonfuls to one pail of water, would act as an effective disinfectant and germicide, and when used as directed would disinfect drains and outdoor vaults and sinks, urinals, and water closets, and would sterilize cuspidors; whereas the article, when used for general disinfection in the dilution of three tablespoonfuls to one pail of water, would not act as an effective disinfectant and germicide, and when used as directed it would not disinfect drains and outdoor vaults and would not disinfect sinks, urinals, and water closets, and would not sterilize cuspidors.

The information also charged a violation of the Federal Caustic Poison Act reported in notice of judgment no. 28, published under that act.

On April 2, 1935, a plea of guilty was entered on behalf of the defendant company and the court imposed a fine of $50 and costs for violation of both acts.

M. L. WILSON, *Acting Secretary of Agriculture.*

1378. Adulteration and misbranding of Pine Disinfectant. U. S. v. Hans V. Jansen (Jansen Soap & Chemical Co.). Plea of guilty. Fine, $75. (I. & F. no. 1670. Sample no. 23753–A.)

This case was based on an interstate shipment of a fungicide which contained a smaller proportion of active ingredients and a larger proportion of inert ingredients than declared on the label. The labeling also bore unwarranted claims regarding the alleged disinfecting properties of the article.

On January 30, 1934, the United States attorney for the Northern District of California, acting upon a report by the Secretary of Agriculture, filed in the district court an information against Hans V. Jansen, trading as the Jansen Soap & Chemical Co., San Francisco, Calif., alleging shipment by said defendant on or about August 24, 1932, from the State of California into the State of Nevada, of a quantity of Pine Disinfectant which was an adulterated and misbranded fungicide within the meaning of the Insecticide Act of 1910.

The article was alleged to be adulterated in that the statements appearing on the label, "Inert, approximate 12% water Total active approximate 88%", represented that its standard and quality were such that it contained not less than 88 percent of active ingredients and not more than 12 percent of inert ingredients, whereas the strength and purity of the article fell below the professed standard and quality under which it was sold, since it contained much less than 88 percent of active ingredients, and contained much more than 12 percent of inert ingredients.

Misbranding was alleged for the reason that the statements. "Inert, Approximately 12% water Total Active Approximate 88%, Disinfectant * * * For Washing Floors, Woodwork, Sinks, Refrigerators, etc.,—three or four teaspoons-ful to a pail of water. * * * For An Aid In Ordinary Disinfection. A proportion of one part to one hundred parts of water", and "Disinfectant * * * For * * * Cesspools, * * * one pint to five gallons of water", borne on the can label, were false and misleading, and by reason of the said statements the article was labeled so as to deceive and mislead the purchaser, since it contained active ingredients in a proportion much less than 88 percent, and contained inert ingredients in a proportion much greater than 12 percent; it would not be an effective disinfectant when used at the dilutions specified on the label; and it would not disinfect cesspools when used as directed.

The information also charged a violation of the Food and Drugs Act reported in notice of judgment no. 24512, published under that act.

On September 16, 1935, the defendant entered a plea of guilty and the court imposed fines on both charges, the fine on the counts charging violation of the Insecticide Act being $75.

M. L. WILSON, *Acting Secretary of Agriculture.*

1379. Adulteration and misbranding of Newco. U. S. v. Milton Newman (Newco Laboratories). Plea of nolo contendere. Fine, $15. (I. &. F. no. 1701. Sample no. 58914–A.)

This case involved a product that contained a smaller proportion of the active ingredient and a larger proportion of inert ingredients than declared on the label. The labeling was further objectionable because of unwarranted claims regarding its alleged disinfectant properties.

On June 11, 1934, the United States attorney for the Eastern District of Pennsylvania, acting upon a report by the Secretary of Agriculture, filed in the district court an information against Milton Newman, trading as the Newco Laboratories, Philadelphia, Pa., alleging shipment by said defendant on or about December 7, 1933, from the State of Pennsylvania into the State of New Jersey, of a quantity of Newco, which was an adulterated and misbranded fungicide within the meaning of the Insecticide Act of 1910.

The article was alleged to be adulterated in that the statements, "Active Ingredient Sodium Hypochlorite 5% by Wt. Inert Ingredients 95% by Wt.", borne on the label, represented that its standard and quality were such that it contained an active ingredient, sodium hypochlorite, in the proportion of 5 percent by weight, and contained inert ingredients, i. e., substances that do not prevent, destroy, repel, or mitigate fungi, in the proportion of not more than 95 percent by weight; whereas the strength and purity of the article fell below the professed standard and quality under which it was sold, since it contained less than 5 percent of sodium hypochlorite by weight, and contained inert ingredients in a proportion greater than 95 percent by weight.

Misbranding was alleged for the reason that the statements, "Active Ingredient Sodium Hypochlorite 5% by Wt. Inert Ingredients 95% by Wt." and "Disinfectant * * * For use on * * * Drain Pipes", were false and misleading, and by reason of the said statements the article was labeled so as to deceive and mislead the purchaser, since it contained an active ingredient, sodium hypochlorite, in a proportion less than 5 percent by weight, and contained inert ingredients in a proportion greater than 95 percent by weight, and it would not disinfect drain pipes when used as directed.

On June 17, 1935, the defendant entered a plea of nolo contendere, and the court imposed a fine of $15.

M. L. WILSON, *Acting Secretary of Agriculture.*

1380. Misbranding of compound larkspur lotion. U. S. v. Richard Gailliard Dunwody. Plea of guilty. Sentence suspended and defendant placed on probation for one year. (I. & F. no. 1705. Sample no. 39968–A.)

This case was based on an interstate shipment of an insecticide that contained undeclared inert ingredients.

On October 12, 1934, the United States attorney for the Northern District of Georgia, acting upon a report by the Secretary of Agriculture, filed in the district court an information against Richard Gailliard Dunwody, trading as R. G. Dunwody & Sons, alleging shipment by said defendant on or about July 20, 1933, from the State of Georgia into the State of Florida, of a quantity of compound larkspur lotion, which was a misbranded insecticide within the meaning of the Insecticide Act of 1910.

The article was alleged to be misbranded in that it consisted partially of inert substances, namely, substances other than alkaloids of larkspur and acetic acid, which substances do not prevent, destroy, repel, or mitigate insects, and the name and percentage amount of each inert ingredient present in the article was not stated plainly and correctly on the bottle label; nor, in lieu thereof, were the name and percentage amount of each substance or ingredient of the article having insecticidal properties, and the total percentage of the inert substances or ingredients, stated plainly and correctly on the label.

On March 13, 1935, the defendant entered a plea of guilty and the court ordered that sentence be suspended and the defendant placed on probation for one year.

M. L. WILSON, *Acting Secretary of Agriculture.*

1381. Adulteration and misbranding of Black Eagle Roach Exterminator. U. S. v. B. & B. Exterminators, Inc. Plea of nolo contendere. Fine, $50 and costs. (I. & F. no. 1729. Sample no. 54575-A.)

This case involved an insecticide that was adulterated and misbranded, since it contained a smaller proportion of active ingredients, and a larger proportion of inert ingredients than declared on the label. The article was further misbranded since the label contained unwarranted claims regarding its effectiveness in the control of insects; and it was represented to be a mild poison and harmless when breathed, whereas it was very poisonous and was harmful if breathed; it contained inert ingredients other than that declared, and was short weight.

On November 9, 1934, the United States attorney for the District of Maryland, acting upon a report by the Secretary of Agriculture, filed in the district court an information against the B. & B. Exterminators, Inc., Baltimore, Md., alleging shipment by said company on or about October 26, 1933, from the State of Maryland into the District of Columbia, of a quantity of Black Eagle Roach Exterminator which was an adulterated and misbranded insecticide, other than Paris green and lead arsenate, within the meaning of the Insecticide Act of 1910.

The article was alleged to be adulterated in that the statement, "Active Matter 90% Inert Matter (flour) 10%", borne on the package label, represented that its standard and quality were such that it contained active matter, i. e., substances that prevent, destroy, repel, or mitigate insects, in the proportion of not less than 90 percent; and contained inert matter, i. e., substances that do not prevent, destroy, repel, or mitigate insects, in the proportion of not more than 10 percent, and that flour was the only inert ingredient; whereas its strength and purity fell below the professed standard and quality under which it was sold, since it contained active matter in a proportion much less than 90 percent, it contained inert matter in a proportion much greater than 10 percent, and it contained inert ingredients other than flour.

Misbranding was alleged for the reason that the statements, "Active Matter 90% Inert Matter (flour) 10%", "Roach Exterminator For Exterminating Roaches and Water Bugs Will Exterminate Roaches or Water Bugs * * * For Exterminating Roaches and Water Bugs * * * The roaches or water bugs will run about very excitedly for two or three hours after the exterminator is applied, * * * It is highly important that a second light application should be made about fifteen days after the first in order to kill any young roaches that may have hatched from an egg sack after the first extermination. This preparation is absolutely guaranteed to exterminate roaches of any kind if used as directed", "This powder is intended for roaches and water bugs, but is a cure-all", "This preparation is mildly toxic to human beings and will cause nausea if taken in any large quantity on food. Therefore food should be covered so that the dust will not settle on it when this powder is being used. However, the small quantity of dust that would settle on food when the powder is being properly used would not do any harm if eaten, in other words this powder may be safely used in kitchens, pantrys, restaurants, at soda fountains or anywhere else. This powder will cause sneezing when dusted into the air, but is absolutely harmless to breathe", "This package contains 8 ounces * * * Contents 8 Oz. Net", borne on the package labels, were false and misleading, and by reason of the said statements the article was labeled so as to deceive and mislead the purchaser, in that they represented that the article contained 90 percent of active matter, and 10 percent of inert matter and that flour was the only inert ingredient; that it would exterminate roaches and water bugs under all conditions; that it was a cure-all; that it was mildly toxic to human beings and was absolutely harmless to breathe; and that each package contained 8 ounces of the article; whereas it contained less than 90 percent of active matter; it contained more than 10 percent of inert matter and contained inert ingredients other than flour; it would not exterminate roaches and water bugs under all conditions when used as directed; it was not a cure-all; it was not mildly toxic to human beings, but was very poisonous and was not absolutely harmless, but would be harmful to human beings if breathed into the system; and the packages contained less than 8 ounces of the article.

On March 15, 1935, a plea of nolo contendere was entered on behalf of the defendant company, and the court imposed a fine of $50 and costs.

M. L. WILSON, *Acting Secretary of Agriculture.*

1382. **Misbranding of Kilrust.   U. S. v. Morris B. Reade, Inc.   Plea of guilty. Fine, $100.**   (I. & F. no. 1730.   Sample no. 26453-A, Dom. no. 42244.)

This case was based on shipments of Kilrust, an insecticide and fungicide which contained a smaller percentage of copper, as metallic, than declared on the label. The labeling was further objectionable because of unwarranted claims regarding the alleged effectiveness of the article in the control of insects and fungi.

On October 23, 1934, the United States attorney for the District of New Jersey, acting upon a report by the Secretary of Agriculture, filed in the district court an information against Morris B. Reade, Inc., Belleville, N. J., alleging shipment by said company on or about March 4, 1932, and March 1, 1933, from the State of New Jersey into the State of Maryland, of quantities of Kilrust which was a misbranded insecticide and fungicide within the meaning of the Insecticide Act of 1910.

The article was alleged to be misbranded in that the statements, "Copper as metallic 1.50%", "Destroys * * * Mealy Bug * * * Red Spider * * * As an Insecticide: For * * * Mealy Bug * * * one part 'Kilrust' to 35 parts water", "Kilrust Combined Fungicide and Insecticide A positive preventive and check of the common forms of Rust on Carnations and Antirrhinum. Black Spot on Roses and some forms of Fungus Diseases. * * * For rust on Carnations, one part 'Kilrust' to 35 parts water; For all other flowers: Antirrhinum, one part of 'Kilrust' to 50 parts of water", borne on the bottle label, were false and misleading, and by reason of the said statements the article was labeled so as to deceive and mislead the purchaser, since it contained copper, as metallic, in a proportion less than 1.50 percent, it would not act as an effective insecticide against red spider and mealy bug, and would not act as a check and positive preventive of the common forms of rust on carnations and antirrhinum, or of black spot on roses, or of the more common forms of fungous diseases of flowers when used as directed.

On January 25, 1935, a plea of guilty was entered on behalf of the defendant company. On April 13, 1935, the court imposed a sentence of a $100 fine.

M. L. WILSON, *Acting Secretary of Agriculture.*

1383. Misbranding of Goshen Glow Shampoo, Dermatone, Mange Relief, and B. I. S. Ointment. U. S. v. J. F. DeVine Laboratories, Inc. Plea of guilty. Fine, $150. (I. & F. nos. 1735, 1754. Sample nos. 43736–A, 43745–A, 65957–A, 65958–A.)

This case involved shipments of Dermatone, Mange Relief, and B. I. S. Ointment the labeling of which contained false and misleading claims regarding the effectiveness of the articles in the control of mange; the labeling of the B. I. S. Ointment also containing unwarranted germicidal claims. The products and a shipment of Goshen Glow Shampoo, also covered by the information, contained undeclared inert ingredients.

On March 29, 1935, the United States attorney for the Southern District of New York, acting upon a report by the Secretary of Agriculture, filed in the district court an information against the J. F. DeVine Laboratories, Inc., New York, N. Y., alleging shipment by said company on or about October 31 and November 14, 1933, from the State of New York into the State of New Jersey of quantities of Goshen Glow Shampoo, Dermatone, and Mange Relief which were misbranded insecticides within the meaning of the Insecticide Act of 1910, and on or about November 6, 1933, from the State of New York into the State of New Jersey of a quantity of B. I. S. Ointment which was a misbranded insecticide and fungicide within the meaning of said act.

The articles were alleged to be misbranded in that they consisted partly of an inert substance, water, which substance does not prevent, destroy, repel, or mitigate insects, and the name and percentage amount of the said inert substance so present therein were not stated plainly and correctly, or at all, on the label; nor, in lieu thereof, were the name and percentage amount of each ingredient of the article having insecticidal properties and the total percentage of the inert substances or ingredients stated plainly and correctly, or at all, on the label.

Misbranding of the Dermatone, Mange Relief, and B. I. S. Ointment was alleged for the further reason that the statements in the labeling, "Dermatone A * * * lotion, recommended particularly for the treatment of demodectic and sarcoptic mange", with respect to the Dermatone, "Mange Relief (Mange Oil)", with respect to the Mange Relief, and "An all around * * * germicidal ointment. Its * * * germicidal * * * properties give it positive merit, * * * as an adjuvant in the treating of demodectic * * * mange", with respect to the B. I. S. Ointment, were false and misleading, and by reason of the said statements the articles were labeled so as to deceive and mislead the purchaser since the Dermatone would not be a satisfactory treatment for demodectic mange of dogs; the Mange Relief would not act as an effective relief for all types and varieties of mange of dogs; and the B. I. S. Ointment was not a germicidal ointment, did not possess germicidal properties, and did not possess value in the treatment of demodectic mange.

The information also charged that the B. I. S. Ointment was misbranded in violation of the Food and Drugs Act reported in notice of judgment no. 24542, published under that act.

On April 15, 1935, a plea of guilty was entered on behalf of the defendant company and the court imposed fines on all charges. The fine assessed on the charge for violation of the Insecticide Act of 1910 was $150.

M. L. WILSON, *Acting Secretary of Agriculture.*

1384. Misbranding of High Jene Deodorizer Moth Killer. U. S. v. John J. Smith (Dovola Co.). Plea of guilty. Fine, $25. (I. & F. no. 1737. Sample no. 65783–A.)

This case involved an insecticide which was misbranded because of unwarranted claims in the labeling regarding its alleged effectiveness in the control of moths, and because it was not composed of chlorine crystals as represented.

On November 16, 1934, the United States attorney for the Northern District of Illinois, acting upon a report by the Secretary of Agriculture, filed in the district court an information against John J. Smith, trading as the Dovola Co., Chicago, Ill., alleging shipment by said defendant on or about March 8, 1934, from the State of Illinois into the State of Missouri of a quantity of High Jene Deodorizer Moth Killer, which was a misbranded insecticide within the meaning of the Insecticide Act of 1910.

The article was alleged to be misbranded in that the statements, "Moth Proofing Chlorine Crystals For * * * Overstuffed Furniture", "Chlorine Crystals", and "Stronger and more effective than anything on the market", borne on the label, were false and misleading, and by reason of the said statements the article was labeled so as to deceive and mislead the purchaser, since it would not act as an effective insecticide against moths in overstuffed furniture, and would not moth-proof furniture when used as directed; it did not consist of chlorine crystals, but did consist of paradichlorobenzene with a small amount of perfume; and it was not stronger and more effective against moths than anything on the market.

On February 18, 1935, the defendant entered a plea of guilty and the court imposed a fine of $25.

M. L. WILSON, *Acting Secretary of Agriculture.*

1385. Misbranding of Havok. U. S. v. Henry & Henry, Inc. Plea of guilty. Fine, $25. (I. & F. no. 1739. Sample no. 58174–A.)

This case involved an interstate shipment of an insecticide which was misbranded because it was represented to be nonpoisonous; whereas it was poisonous.

On December 10, 1934, the United States attorney for the Western District of New York, acting upon a report by the Secretary of Agriculture, filed in the district court an information against Henry & Henry, Inc., Buffalo, N. Y., alleging shipment by said company on or about October 17, 1933, from the State of New York into the State of Massachusetts of a quantity of Havok which was a misbranded insecticide within the meaning of the Insecticide Act of 1910.

The article was alleged to be misbranded in that the statement "Non-Poisonous", borne on the label, was false and misleading, and by reason of the said statement the article was labeled so as to deceive and mislead the purchaser, since it represented that the article was nonpoisonous, whereas it was poisonous.

On March 15, 1935, a plea of guilty was entered on behalf of the defendant company and the court imposed a fine of $25.

M. L. WILSON, *Acting Secretary of Agriculture.*

1386. Misbranding of Germ-X. U. S. v. American Lanolin Corporation. Plea of nolo contendere. Fine, $1. (I. & F. no. 1741. Sample no. 68357–A.)

This case was based on an interstate shipment of a product which was misbranded because of unwarranted claims regarding its alleged effectiveness as a disinfectant and sterilizer, and its alleged effectiveness to kill hog lice. The label was further objectionable, since the product was represented to contain no poison and to be harmless, whereas it contained a poison and was not harmless.

On February 21, 1935, the United States attorney for the District of Massachusetts, acting upon a report by the Secretary of Agriculture, filed in the district court an information against the American Lanolin Corporation, Lawrence, Mass., alleging shipment by said company on or about February 13, 1934, from the State of Massachusetts into the State of New Hampshire, of a quantity of Germ-X, which was a misbranded insecticide and fungicide within the meaning of the Insecticide Act of 1910.

The article was alleged to be misbranded in that the following statements appearing in the labeling, "Disinfectant * * * General Cleaning: When washing floors, paints, windows, glasses, dishes, etc., use one tablespoonful to a gallon of water. * * * Floors, Kitchen tables, Cupboards, etc., Wash thoroughly with dilution of two tablespoonfuls to a quart of water", "Disinfectant * * * Milk Bottles:—Wash and brush with hot water and soda and thoroughly rinse with Germ-X Solution 'C', Pails, Cans, Etc.:—Wash with hot water and soda and thoroughly rinse with Germ-X Solution 'C'. Allow to dry without wiping. * * * Refrigerators:—After washing and scrubbing spray thoroughly over walls, floors and shelves with Solution 'C' * * * Cheese Factory:—Solution 'C' should be used freely for moulds, presses and utensils as an aid after washing and scrubbing in keeping them sweet and clean. * * * Keep barns and stables clean by spraying with Solution 'G' at least once a week. At the same time wash or spray mangers and drinking utensils with Solution 'A'. * * * Poultry * * * Spray roosts and dropping boards with Solution 'F'. Wash all drinking utensils with Solution 'A'. * * * Thoroughly wash and disinfect incubators and brooders with Solution 'G.' Do this between each hatch. * * * The housewife who uses this powerful germicide in her wash water will always have a clean and sanitary home. * * * In washing Floors and Walls—One tablespoon Germ-X should be put right in with the washing water when floors or walls, especially marbles, tiles and concrete, are to be cleaned", "General power to destroy germs. * * * Germ-X the germ killer * * * Keep milk sweet and clean by adding a few drops of Germ-X to each quart. * * * Bed linen and similar articles that have been used in sick rooms should always be sterilized with Germ-X in the washing process—two tablespoons to tub of water. In the Kitchen—Germ-X is most effective in sterilizing * * * Garbage cans and sinks * * * and also makes for sterile conditions. It acts as a disinfectant for drain pipes and traps. * * * In the Bathroom—Germ-X * * * it drives out, kills bacteria quickly and effectively", "As absolute proof of its harmlessness Germ-X * * * The fact that it contains no poison", "Solution 'A' sprayed on animals will kill hog lice", were false and misleading, and by reason of the said statements the article was labeled so as to deceive and mislead the purchaser, since it would not disinfect floors, paints, windows, glasses, dishes, etc.; would not disinfect kitchen tables, cupboards, etc., when used as directed; it would not act as an effective disinfectant when used in the dilutions specified; it would not sterilize milk, bed linen, and similar articles that have been used in sick rooms, garbage cans and sinks, drain pipes and traps, and articles in bathrooms, when used as directed; it was not harmless and did contain a poison; and would not kill hog lice when used as directed.

The information also charged violations of the Food and Drugs Act reported in notice of judgment no. 24540, published under that act.

On March 25, 1935, a plea of nolo contendere was entered on behalf of the defendant company, and the court imposed fines on all charges, the fine on the count charging violation of the Insecticide Act of 1910, being $1.

M. L. WILSON, *Acting Secretary of Agriculture.*

1387. Misbranding of Handy Plantox. U. S. v. Clean Home Products, Inc. Plea of guilty. Fine, $25. (I. & F. no. 1743. Sample no. 36310–A.)

This case involved a product which was misbranded because of unwarranted claims in the labeling regarding its alleged insecticidal properties. The labeling was further objectionable, since the article was represented to be harmless to humans and animals, whereas it contained a poisonous substance.

On January 16, 1935, the United States attorney for the Northern District of Illinois, acting upon a report by the Secretary of Agriculture, filed in the district court an information against the Clean Home Products, Inc., trading at Chicago, Ill., alleging shipment by said company on or about May 19, 1933, from the State of Illinois into the State of Wisconsin of a quantity of Handy

Plantox, which was a misbranded insecticide within the meaning of the Insecticide Act of 1910.

The article was alleged to be misbranded in that the statements, "Plantox is the easy and sure way to kill many leaf-eating or chewing insects, including the following: * * * Red Spider * * * Grape Berry Moth * * * Oriental Fruit Moth", "Handy Plantox Death to most insect pests", "Handy Plantox Harmless to Humans or Animals", borne on the package label, were false and misleading, and by reason of the said statements the article was labeled so as to deceive and mislead the purchaser, since it would not kill red spiders, grape berry moths, and oriental fruit moths; would not act as an effective insecticide against most insect pests when used as directed; and it was not harmless to humans and animals, but did contain a poisonous substance.

On March 28, 1935, a plea of guilty was entered on behalf of the defendant company and the court imposed a fine of $25.

M. L. WILSON, *Acting Secretary of Agriculture.*

1388. Adulteration and misbranding of Pestroy. U. S. v. The Sherwin-Williams Co. Plea of guilty. Fine, $25. (I. & F. no. 1748. Sample nos. 67902–A, 67914–A.)

This case was based on an interstate shipment of a product that contained less active ingredients, less arsenate of lead, less total arsenic, and a larger percentage of inert ingredients than declared on the label. The labeling was further objectionable because of unwarranted claims regarding the alleged effectiveness of the article in the control of insects.

On January 7, 1935, the United States attorney for the Northern District of Illinois, acting upon a report by the Secretary of Agriculture, filed in the district court an information against the Sherwin-Williams Co., trading at Chicago, Ill., alleging shipment by said company on or about February 25, 1934, from the State of Illinois into the State of New York of a quantity of Pestroy which was an adulterated and misbranded insecticide, other than Paris green and lead arsenate, and fungicide within the meaning of the Insecticide Act of 1910.

The article was alleged to be adulterated in that the statements, "Total Active Ingredients 25.5% Arsenate of Lead 14.5% Total Arsenic (expressed as percentum of Metallic Arsenic) not less than 2.80% Inert Ingredients 74.5%", borne on the can label, represented that its standard and quality were such that it contained total active ingredients in the proportion of not less than 25.5 percent; contained arsenate of lead in the proportion of not less than 14.5 percent; contained arsenic (expressed as percentum of metallic arsenic) in the proportion of not less than 2.80 percent; and contained inert ingredients in the proportion of not more than 74.5 percent; whereas the strength and purity of the article fell below the professed standard and quality under which it was sold, since it contained less than 25.5 percent of total active ingredients, it contained less than 14.5 percent of arsenate of lead, it contained less than 2.80 percent of total arsenic (expressed as percentum of metallic arsenic), and contained more than 74.5 percent of inert ingredients.

Misbranding was alleged for the reason that the above-quoted statements borne on the can label were false and misleading, and by reason of the said statements the article was labeled so as to deceive and mislead the purchaser, since it contained less total active ingredients, less arsenate of lead, less arsenic (expressed as percentum of metallic arsenic), and a larger percentage of inert ingredients than declared on the label. Misbranding was alleged for the further reason that the following statements, "Pestroy A combination of arsenate of lead and Bordeaux mixture in dry form for certain fruit tree and garden spraying * * * for the control of certain chewing insects * * * of apple, pear, certain variety of plums, currant, gooseberry, grape and strawberry, also bean, beet, cabbage, cauliflower, eggplant, tomato, cucumber, watermelon, muskmelon, squash, use from 7 to 9½ pounds of Pestroy to 50 gallons of water or 7 to 9 level tablespoonfuls to 1 gallon of water. For potato, use 12 pounds of Pestroy to 50 gallons of water or 12 level tablespoonfuls to 1 gallon of water. Pestroy also may be applied as a dust against the insects named. When used in this way it should be applied just as it comes from the package and care taken to distribute it evenly over the plants", borne on the label, were false and misleading, and by reason of the said statements the article was labeled so as to deceive and mislead the purchaser in that they represented that the article would act as an effective control against the insects that infest or attack the above-named plants and trees; whereas it would not act as an effective control against a majority of the insects commonly found infesting or attacking the said plants and trees, when used as directed.

On February 18, 1935, a plea of guilty was entered on behalf of the defendant company and the court imposed a fine of $25.

                    M. L. WILSON, *Acting Secretary of Agriculture.*

1389. Adulteration and misbranding of Reliable Roach and Ant Destroyer. U. S. v. Henry J. Edwards (Whippet Sales Co.). Plea of nolo contendere. Fine, $10.   (I. & F. no. 1749.   Sample no. 71749–A.)

This case involved an insecticide which contained active ingredients in a proportion much less, and inert ingredients in a proportion much greater, than those declared on the label.

On January 4, 1935, the United States attorney for the District of Massachusetts, acting upon a report by the Secretary of Agriculture, filed in the district court an information against Henry J. Edwards, trading as the Whippet Sales Co., Boston, Mass., alleging shipment and delivery for shipment by said defendant, on or about May 7, 1934, from the State of Massachusetts into the State of Rhode Island, of a quantity of Reliable Roach and Ant Destroyer which was an adulterated and misbranded insecticide within the meaning of the Insecticide Act of 1910.

The article was alleged to be adulterated in that the statements, "Active Ingredient, Sodium Fluoride 50% Inert Ingredient 50%", borne on the carton label, represented that it contained an active ingredient, sodium fluoride, in the proportion of not less than 50 percent, and contained an inert substance in the proportion of not more than 50 percent; whereas the strength and purity of the article fell below the professed standard and quality under which it was sold, since it contained sodium fluoride in a proportion much less than 50 percent and contained an inert substance or ingredient in a proportion much greater than 50 percent.

Misbranding was alleged for the reason that the statements, "Active Ingredient, Sodium Fluoride 50% Inert Ingredient 50%", borne on the label, were false and misleading, and by reason of the said statements the article was labeled so as to deceive and mislead the purchaser, since it contained sodium fluoride in a proportion much less than 50 percent, and contained an inert ingredient in a proportion much greater than 50 percent.

On April 8, 1935, the defendant entered a plea of nolo contendere, and the court imposed a fine of $10.

                    M. L. WILSON, *Acting Secretary of Agriculture.*

1390. Misbranding of Old Nick's Seed Treatment.   U. S. v. Ivan James Nickerson (Old Nick Seed Treatment Co.).   Plea of guilty.   Fine, $50.   (I. & F. no. 1750.   Sample no. 41534–A.)

This case involved an insecticide the labeling of which contained unwarranted claims regarding its alleged effectiveness in the control of certain insects. The labeling was further objectionable since the product was represented to be nonpoisonous, whereas it was poisonous.

On March 14, 1935, the United States attorney for the Western District of Missouri, acting upon a report by the Secretary of Agriculture, filed in the district court an information against Ivan James Nickerson, trading as the Old Nick Seed Treatment Co., Pattonsburg, Mo., alleging shipment by said defendant on or about May 15, 1933, from the State of Missouri into the State of Iowa, of a quantity of Old Nick's Seed Treatment which was a misbranded insecticide within the meaning of the Insecticide Act of 1910.

The article was alleged to be misbranded in that the statements appearing in the labeling, "Absolutely protects corn from * * * wire worms or any pest that attacks seed in the ground" and "Non-Poisonous", were false and misleading, and by reason of the said statements the article was labeled so as to deceive and mislead the purchaser, since they represented that the article, when used as directed, would protect corn against wire worms and any pest that attacks seed in the ground, and that it was nonpoisonous; whereas it would not protect corn against wire worms, nor would it protect corn against all other pests when used as directed on the label, and the article was poisonous.

On June 17, 1935, the defendant entered a plea of guilty and the court imposed a fine of $50.

                    M. L. WILSON, *Acting Secretary of Agriculture.*

1391. Misbranding of Industrial Pine Disinfectant. U. S. v. Ira M. Lippel (Industrial Laboratories. Plea of guilty. Fine, $25 and costs. (I. & F. no. 1752. Sample no. 62260–A.)

This case was based on an interstate shipment of a product sold as a germicide which was misbranded because of unwarranted claims in the labeling regarding its alleged effectiveness as a disinfectant. The labeling was further objectionable since the article was represented to be nontoxic, whereas it was not nontoxic.

On January 17, 1935, the United States attorney for the District of Maryland, acting upon a report by the Secretary of Agriculture, filed in the district court an information against Ira M. Lippel, trading as the Industrial Laboratories, Baltimore, Md., alleging shipment by said defendant on or about May 4, 1934, from the State of Maryland into the State of West Virginia, of a quantity of Industrial Pine Disinfectant which was a misbranded fungicide within the meaning of the Insecticide Act of 1910.

The article was alleged to be misbranded in that the following statements appearing in the labeling, "It is non-toxic", "Pine Disinfectant has certain advantages over many other common disinfectants * * * it is more effective", "Disinfectant * * * For Drip Machines use a 4% solution. Disinfectant * * * It is valuable for use in Drainage Pipes. Pour 3 to 4 ounces of full strength Pine Disinfectant into the pipes several times each week. For Disinfecting Rooms, use the full strength Pine Disinfectant in open pans and allow to stand", were false and misleading, and by reason of the said statements the article was labeled so as to deceive and mislead the purchaser, since they represented that the article was nontoxic and was more effective than many common disinfectants, that the said article would disinfect when used in drip machines in a 4-percent dilution, and when used as directed would disinfect drainage pipes and rooms; whereas the article was not nontoxic, it was not more effective than many common disinfectants, it would not disinfect when used in drip machines in a 4-percent dilution, and would not disinfect drainage pipes and rooms when used as directed.

The information also charged a violation of the Food and Drugs Act reported in notice of judgment no. 24541, published under that act.

On February 7, 1935, the defendant entered a plea of guilty and the court imposed a fine of $25 and costs on each charge.

M. L. WILSON, *Acting Secretary of Agriculture.*

1392. Adulteration and misbranding of Sparco Insect Powder. U. S. v. Charles B. Fretwell. Plea of nolo contendere. Fine, $25. (I. & F. no. 1753. Sample no. 49221–A.)

This case involved a product that was adulterated and misbranded since it contained a smaller proportion of sodium fluoride and a larger proportion of inert ingredients than declared on the label. The article was further misbranded since it contained inert ingredients other than that declared, it was labeled with unwarranted claims regarding its alleged effectiveness in the control of certain insects, and failed to bear on the label a declaration of the inert ingredients.

On December 17, 1934, the United States attorney for the Western District of South Carolina, acting upon a report by the Secretary of Agriculture, filed in the district court an information against Charles B. Fretwell, trading as the Sparco Laboratories, Spartanburg, S. C., alleging shipment by said defendant on or about September 1, 1933, from the State of South Carolina into the State of Florida of a quantity of Sparco Insect Powder which was an adulterated and misbranded insecticide, other than Paris green and lead arsenate, within the meaning of the Insecticide Act of 1910.

The article was alleged to be adulterated in that the statements, "Contains Sodium Fluoride 66% Talc 34%", borne on the package label, represented that its standard and quality were such that it contained sodium fluoride in the proportion of not less than 66 percent, and contained talc in the proportion of 34 percent; whereas the strength and purity of the article fell below the professed standard and quality under which it was sold, since it contained less than 66 percent of sodium fluoride, it contained less than 34 percent of talc, and it contained further inorganic impurities in addition to talc.

Misbranding was alleged for the reason that the statements, "Contains Sodium Fluoride 66% Talc 34%" and "For * * * Mites, Sticktight Fleas * * * Household Use. For * * * other insects, thoroughly dust the cracks and other places used by the insects", borne on the package label, were false and misleading, and by reason of the said statements the article was labeled so as to deceive and mislead the purchaser, since it contained less than 66 percent of sodium fluoride, it contained more than 34 percent of talc, it contained inorganic impurities in addition to talc, and it would not act as an effective insecticide against mites, sticktight fleas, and all other insects when used as directed. Misbranding was alleged for the further reason that the article consisted partly of inert substances, namely, substances other than sodium fluoride, which inert substances do not prevent, destroy, repel, or mitigate insects, and the name and percentage amount of each of the inert substances present in the article were not plainly and correctly stated on the package label; nor, in lieu thereof, were the name and percentage amount of each ingredient of the article having insecticidal properties, and the total percentage of the inert substances present therein, stated plainly and correctly on the label.

On February 19, 1935, the defendant entered a plea of nolo contendere, and the court imposed a fine of $25.

M. L. WILSON, *Acting Secretary of Agriculture.*

1393. Misbranding of Cedar Vaporator. U. S. v. Galree Products Co. (Regal Products Co.) Morris S. Galler, and Eugene J. Reefer. Pleas of guilty. Fines, $150. (I. & F. no. 1756. Sample no. 71640.)

This case involved an insecticide which was misbranded because of nuwarranted claims in the labeling regarding its alleged effectiveness in the control of moths.

On February 28, 1935, the United States attorney for the Southern District of New York, acting upon a report by the Secretary of Agriculture, filed in the district court an information against the Galree Products Co., a corporation, also trading under the name of the Regal Products Co., and Morris S. Galler and Eugene J. Reefer, New York, N. Y., alleging shipment by said defendants on or about May 1, 1934, from the State of New York into the State of Massachusetts, of a quantity of Cedar Vaporator, which was a misbranded insecticide within the meaning of the Insecticide Act of 1910.

The article was alleged to be misbranded in that the following statements appearing in the labeling, (carton) "Cedar Vaporator Kills Moths Cedarizes for 12 Months * * * Important For real moth protection use 'Cedar Vaporator' in every closet. * * * Use in space as large as 75 cubic feet" and (bottle) "Cedar Vaporator Kills Moths Cedarizes for 12 Months * * * Directions Read Carefully. 1. Remove the bottle carefully from the metal holder. 2. Punch hole in center of bottle cap. Be sure the liquid is clearly visible through this hole. 3. Hang the metal holder on the baseboard of clothes closet. 4. Replace bottle in metal holder, press down as far as possible so that the bottle sets solidly in the holder. Use in space as large as 75 cubic feet. To confine fumes, keep doors closed", were false and misleading, and by reason of the said statements the article was labeled so as to deceive and mislead the purchaser, since they represented that the article, when used as directed, would kill moths and would act as an effective insecticide against moths for 12 months; whereas it would not kill moths and would not act as an effective insecticide against moths for 12 months when used as directed.

On April 8, 1935, the defendants entered pleas of guilty, and the court imposed fines totaling $150.

M. L. WILSON, *Acting Secretary of Agriculture.*

1394. Misbranding of Pet Dry Bath Powder. U. S. v. General Desserts Corporation. Plea of guilty. Fine, $25. (I. & F. no. 1757. Sample no. 71761–A.)

This case involved an insecticide which contained inert ingredients that were not declared on the label.

On March 5, 1935, the United States attorney for the Southern District of New York, acting upon a report by the Secretary of Agriculture, filed in the district court an information against the General Desserts Corporation, New York, N. Y., alleging shipment by said company on or about June 7, 1934, from the State of New York into the State of Massachusetts of a quantity of Pet Dry Bath Powder, which was a misbranded insecticide within the meaning of the Insecticide Act of 1910.

The article was alleged to be misbranded in that it consisted partly of inert substances, namely, substances other than naphthalene and powdered pyrethrum flowers, and the name and percentage amount of each inert ingredient of the article were not stated plainly or correctly, or at all, on the carton label; nor, in lieu thereof, were the name and percentage amount of each substance or ingredient of the article having insecticidal properties, and the total percentage of the inert substances or ingredients present therein stated plainly or correctly, or at all, on the label.

On April 8 1935, a plea of guilty was entered on behalf of the defendant company and the court imposed a fine of $25.

M. L. WILSON, *Acting Secretary of Agriculture.*

1395. Misbranding of Merax Mercury Cyanide Solution. U. S. v. Dental Research Laboratories and Sales Corporation. Plea of guilty. Fine, $40. (I. & F. no. 1758. Sample no. 48964–A.)

This case involved a product which was misbranded because of unwarranted claims in the labeling regarding its alleged sterilizing properties. The labeling was further objectionable, since it conveyed the misleading impression that borax is effective in the control of fungi, and since the inert ingredients present in the article were not declared.

On January 18, 1935, the United States attorney for the District of Oregon, acting upon a report by the Secretary of Agriculture, filed in the district court an information against the Dental Research Laboratories and Sales Corporation, Portland, Oreg., alleging shipment by said company on or about January 22, 1934, from the State of Oregon into the State of Washington, of a quantity of Merax Mercury Cyanide Solution, which was a misbranded fungicide within the meaning of the Insecticide Act of 1910.

The article was alleged to be misbranded in that the statements, "Active Ingredients Mercury Cyanide 2.63% Borax 3.76%", borne on the bottle label, represented that borax was contained in the article as an active ingredient, that is to say, that it would prevent, destroy, repel, or mitigate fungi; whereas borax was not contained in the article as an active ingredient, since it would not prevent, destroy, repel, or mitigate fungi. Misbranding was alleged for the further reason that the following statements on the bottle label, "A Sterilizing Solution for Surgeon and Dentist * * * To sterilize cutting instruments, cystoscopes, bougies, sounds, rubber catheters, urethral catheters, rubber gloves, needles, syringes, dental hand pieces, scalers, brushers, etc., first clean the instruments thoroughly, the same as you would for boiling; then immerse in the solution from two to five minutes after which they are ready for use. Cutting edges and articles of rubber are not impaired by the solution, diluted or undiluted. * * * Do not sterilize aluminum instruments in Merax Mercury Cyanide Solution as mercury affects aluminum", were false and misleading, and by reason of said statements the article was labeled so as to deceive and mislead the purchaser, since they represented that the article, when used as directed, would sterilize instruments and the articles specified in the label; whereas it would not sterilize instruments and other articles specified in the said label, when used as directed. Misbranding was alleged for the further reason that the article consisted partially of inert substances, and the name and percentage amount of each of the inert substances present in the article were not stated plainly and correctly on the bottle label; nor, in lieu thereof, were the name and percentage amount of each ingredient of the article having fungicidal (bactericidal) properties, and the total percentage of the inert substances present in the article stated plainly and correctly on the bottle label.

On April 25, 1935, a plea of guilty was entered on behalf of the defendant company and the court imposed a fine of $40.

M. L. WILSON, *Acting Secretary of Agriculture.*

1396. Misbranding of Vapoo. U. S. v. 288 Packages and 72 Packages of Vapoo. Default decree of condemnation and destruction. (I. & F. no. 1759. Sample nos. 4900–B, 14201–B.)

This case involved a product which was misbranded because of unwarranted claims in the labeling regarding its alleged disinfectant properties and its effectiveness in the control of moths. The label failed to bear a statement indicating the active and inert ingredients.

On November 22, 1934, the United States attorney for the District of Maryland, acting upon a report by the Secretary of Agriculture, filed in the district court a libel praying seizure and condemnation of 360 packages of Vapoo at Baltimore, Md., alleging that the article had been shipped in interstate commerce on or about August 21 and September 28, 1934, by the Vapoo Products

Co., Inc., from New York, N. Y., and charging misbranding in violation of the Insecticide Act of 1910.

The article was alleged to be misbranded in that the statements, "The Vapoo Shampoo for rugs and upholstery cleans, brightens, disinfects and moth-proofs in one operation", "Cleans, moth-proofs and disinfects", "The Vapoo Shampoo for rugs and upholstery cleans, brightens and disinfects in one operation", "Cleans, disinfects", "The Vapoo Shampoo for * * * upholstery * * * kills moths * * * for upholstery * * * chairs, studio couches, sofa pillows", "The wonder cleaner * * * kills moths * * * can be used on * * * upholstered furniture, mattresses * * * sofa pillows * * * automobile upholstery * * * upholstered chairs, divans, sofas, mattresses, auto upholstery, etc.", appearing in the labeling, were false and misleading, and by reason of the said statements the article was labeled so as to deceive and mislead the purchaser, since the said statements represented that the article when used as directed would disinfect rugs and upholstery and render them moth-proof, and would act as an effective insecticide against moths infesting upholstery, mattresses, sofa pillows, automobile upholstery, divans and sofas; whereas the article when used as directed would not disinfect rugs and upholstery and would not render them moth-proof, would not act as an effective insecticide against moths infesting upholstery, mattresses, sofa pillows, automobile upholstery, divans, and sofas. Misbranding was alleged for the further reason that the article consisted partially of inert substances, i. e., substances other than cedar oils, phenols, soap and double phosphate, and fluoride of sodium, and the name and percentage amount of each inert ingredient present in the article were not plainly and correctly stated on the carton label; nor, in lieu thereof, were the name and percentage amount of each substance or ingredient of the article having insecticidal or fungicidal properties, and the total percentage of the inert substances or ingredients so present therein, stated plainly and correctly on the label.

On March 1, 1935, no claimant appearing, judgment of condemnation was entered and it was ordered that the product be destroyed.

M. L. WILSON, *Acting Secretary of Agriculture.*

1397. Adulteration and misbranding of Niagara Viti Dust. U. S. v. Niagara Sprayer & Chemical Co., Inc. Plea of guilty. Fine, $100. (I. & F. no. 1764. Sample no. 71666–A.)

This case involved a product that was adulterated and misbranded, since it contained a smaller proportion of monohydrated copper sulphate, a smaller proportion of copper (as metallic), and a larger proportion of inert ingredients than declared on the label.

On January 14, 1935, the United States attorney for the Western District of New York, acting upon a report by the Secretary of Agriculture, filed in the district court an information against the Niagara Sprayer & Chemical Co., Inc., Middleport, N. Y., alleging shipment by said company on or about April 20, 1934, from the State of New York into the State of Massachusetts of a quantity of Niagara Viti Dust, which was an adulterated and misbranded insecticide, other than Paris green and lead arsenate, and a fungicide, within the meaning of the Insecticide Act of 1910.

The article was alleged to be adulterated in that the statements, "Mono-Hydrated Copper Sulphate not less than 11.00% Inert Ingredients not over 74.00% Copper (as metallic) not less than 3.94% * * * (Equivalent in Copper Sulphate crystals 15.5%)", borne on the drums containing the article, represented that it contained monohydrated copper sulphate in the proportion of not less than 11 percent, contained inert ingredients in a proportion not greater than 74 percent, contained copper, as metallic, in a proportion of not less than 3.94 percent, and contained not less than the equivalent of 15.5 percent of copper sulphate crystals; whereas the strength and purity of the article fell below the professed standard and quality under which it was sold, since it contained less than 11 percent of monohydrated copper sulphate, it contained more than 74 percent of inert ingredients, it contained less than 3.94 percent of copper, as metallic, and contained less than the equivalent of 15.5 percent of copper sulphate crystals.

Misbranding was alleged for the reason that the above-quoted statements borne on the label were false and misleading, and by reason of the said statements the article was labeled so as to deceive and mislead the purchaser, since it contained less than 11 percent of monohydrated copper sulphate, it contained more than 74 percent of inert ingredients, it contained less than

3.94 percent of copper, as metallic, and contained less than the equivalent of 15.5 percent of copper sulphate crystals.

On June 7, 1935, a plea of guilty was entered on behalf of the defendant company and the court imposed a fine of $100.

M. L. WILSON, *Acting Secretary of Agriculture.*

1398. Adulteration and misbranding of Double-Duty Spray. U. S. v. Devoe & Raynolds Co., Inc. Plea of guilty. Fine, $75. (I. & F. no. 1765. Sample no. 36568–A.)

This case involved a product which was adulterated and misbranded, since it contained a smaller proportion of arsenate of lead, a smaller proportion of total arsenic (expressed as metallic), and a larger proportion of inert ingredients than declared on the label. The article was further misbranded because of unwarranted claims in the labeling regarding its alleged effectiveness against certain insects.

On February 6, 1935, the United States attorney for the Northern District of Illinois, acting upon a report by the Secretary of Agriculture, filed in the district court an information against the Devoe & Raynolds Co., Inc., trading at Chicago, Ill., alleging shipment by said company on or about June 8, 1933, from the State of Illinois into the State of Wisconsin of a quantity of Double-Duty Spray which was an adulterated and misbranded insecticide other than Paris green and lead arsenate, and a fungicide, within the meaning of the Insecticide Act of 1910.

The article was alleged to be adulterated in that the statements, "Arsenate of Lead 15.0% * * * Inert Ingredients 74.0% Total Arsenic (expressed as Metallic Arsenic) not less than 2.9%", borne on the package label, represented that it contained not less than 15 percent of arsenate of lead, not more than 74 percent of inert ingredients, and not less than 2.9 percent of total arsenic (expressed as metallic arsenic); whereas the strength and purity of the article fell below the professed standard and quality under which it was sold, since it contained much less than 15 percent of arsenate of lead, it contained much more than 74 percent of inert ingredients, and it contained much more total arsenic (expressed as metallic arsenic) in a proportion much less than 2.9 percent.

Misbranding was alleged for the reason that the statements, "Arsenate of Lead 15.0% * * * Inert Ingredients 74.0% Total Arsenic (expressed as Metallic Arsenic) not less than 2.9%", "Double-Duty Spray Insecticide * * * For Spraying certain fruits or berries such as grapes, currants and gooseberries and such vegetables as potatoes, use 9 to 9½ pounds Devoe Double Duty Spray to 50 gallons of water, or 9 to 9½ tablespoonsful to 1 gallon of water. For strawberries, tomatoes, beets, cucumbers, eggplant, pears, peppers: use 7 pounds of Devoe Double Duty Spray to 50 gallons of water, or 7 to 8 tablespoonsful to 1 gallon of water. Seven pounds of Devoe Double Duty Spray to 50 gallons of water will produce a mixture containing approximately 1 pound of Arsenate of Lead and a standard 3–3–50 Bordeaux Mixture, which will control effectively certain chewing insects and many fungous diseases of the above fruits and vegetables. If a stronger mixture is desired, use 9½ pounds of Devoe Double Duty Spray to 50 gallons of water, which will give a combination containing approximately 1½ pounds of Arsenate of Lead and a standard 4–4–50 Bordeaux Mixture", borne on the package label, were false and misleading, and by reason of the said statements the article was labeled so as to deceive and mislead the purchaser, since the article contained much less than 15 percent of arsenate of lead, it contained much more than 74 percent of inert ingredients, it contained much less than 2.9 percent of total arsenic (expressed as metallic arsenic), and it would not act as an effective insecticide against chewing insects that infest or attack the fruits and vegetables named on the label, when used as directed.

On March 28, 1935, a plea of guilty was entered on behalf of the defendant company and the court imposed a fine of $75.

M. L. WILSON, *Acting Secretary of Agriculture.*

1399. Adulteration and misbranding of liquor cresol compound and compound solution of cresol. U. S. v. James Good, Inc. Plea of nolo contendere. Fine, $25. (I. & F. no. 1767. Sample nos. 44182–A, 68917–A.)

This case involved a product which was sold under a name recognized in the United States Pharmacopoeia and differed from the standard established by that authority, since other oil or other fatty material, had been substituted for linseed oil. One of the lots contained water in excess of the amount declared on the label.

On March 15, 1935, the United States attorney for the Eastern District of Pennsylvania, acting upon a report by the Secretary of Agriculture, filed in the district court an information against James Good, Inc., trading at Philadelphia, Pa., alleging that said defendant had shipped in interstate commerce on or about October 5, 1933, from the State of Pennsylvania into the District of Columbia, a quantity of a product, labeled "Liquor Cresol Compound U. S. P.", which was adulterated and misbranded in violation of the Insecticide Act of 1910. The information further charged that on or about November 11, 1932, the defendant company sold and delivered under a written guaranty that it was not adulterated and misbranded, a quantity of Liquor Cresol Compound U. S. P.; that on or about January 18, 1934, a portion of the said article, without having been altered in any manner, had been shipped in interstate commerce by the purchaser, from Philadelphia, Pa., into the State of New Jersey, under the label, "Compound Solution of Cresol U. S. P.", that the article was adulterated and misbranded in violation of the Insecticide Act of 1910; and that the defendant, by reason of the said adulteration and misbranding and said guaranty, was amenable to the prosecution and penalties which, but for the guaranty, would have attached to the shipper.

The article was alleged to be adulterated in that the statements appearing on the labels, "Liquor Cresol Compound U. S. P. * * * Water not over 15.00%", with respect to the product in one shipment, and the statement, "Compound Solution of Cresol U. S. P.", with respect to the product in the remaining shipment, represented that the article had been manufactured according to the specifications of the United States Pharmacopoeia, whereas its strength and purity fell below the professed standard and quality under which it was sold, since it did not contain the ingredients specified in the pharmacopoeia, but other oil or other fatty material had been used in the place of linseed oil, and a portion of the product contained more than 15 percent of water.

Misbranding was alleged for the reason that the statements, "Liquor Cresol Compound U. S. P. * * * Water not over 15.00%" and "Compound Solution of Cresol U. S. P.", were false and misleading, and by reason of the said statements the article was labeled so as to deceive and mislead the purchaser in that it was not composed of the ingredients laid down in the pharmacopoeia, since other oil or other fatty material had been substituted for linseed oil, one of the ingredients specified in the United States Pharmacopoeia, and the product in one shipment contained more water than specified in the pharmacopoeia.

On June 21, 1935, a plea of nolo contendere was entered on behalf of the defendant company and the court imposed a fine of $25.

M. L. WILSON, *Acting Secretary of Agriculture.*

1400. Misbranding of Fleavex, My-T-Mite Powder, and Dr. Brehm's Hartz Mountain Antiseptic Bird Wash. U. S. v. The Hartz Mountain Products Co. Plea of guilty. Fine, $130. (I. & F. no. 1768. Sample nos. 65977–A, 65978–A, 65979–A.)

This case was based on interstate shipments of two insecticides, Fleavex and My-T-Mite Powder, and an insecticide and fungicide, Antiseptic Bird Wash. The products in all shipments were misbranded because of short weight and failure to declare the inert ingredients present. The Fleavex and Bird Wash were further misbranded because the former was represented to be non-poisonous, but in fact was poisonous, and the labeling of the latter contained unwarranted antiseptic claims.

On April 5, 1935, the United States attorney for the Southern District of New York, acting upon a report by the Secretary of Agriculture, filed in the district court an information against the Hartz Mountain Products Co., a corporation, New York, N. Y., alleging shipment by said company, in violation of the Insecticide Act of 1910, on or about October 6 and October 26, 1933, from the State of New York into the State of New Jersey of quantities of My-T-Mite Powder, Fleavex, and Dr. Brehm's Hartz Mountain Antiseptic Bird Wash which were misbranded.

The articles were alleged to be misbranded in that the statements, "Net Weight three ounces" and "Non-Poisonous", with respect to the Fleavex, "Net Weight 1 Oz.", with respect to the My-T-Mite Powder, and "2 Oz. Net" and "Antiseptic", with respect to the bird wash, borne on the labels, were false and misleading, and by reason of the said statements the articles were labeled so as to deceive and mislead the purchaser, since the packages contained less than so labeled, the Fleavex was not nonpoisonous and the Bird Wash was not an antiseptic when used as directed. Misbranding was alleged for the further reason that the articles consisted partially of inert substances, namely, powdered pyrethrum stems, sand, and the inactive portion of powdered derris root in the case of the Fleavex and the My-T-Mite Powder; and water in the case of the bird wash; and the name and percentage amount of each inert substance so present in the articles were not stated plainly and correctly on the labels; nor, in lieu thereof, were the name and percentage amount of each substance having insecticidal or fungicidal properties, and the total percentage of the inert substance plainly and correctly stated on the labels.

The information also charged that the antiseptic bird wash was misbranded in violation of the Food and Drugs Act reported in notice of judgment no. 24543, published under that act.

On April 12, 1935, a plea of guilty was entered on behalf of the defendant company and the court imposed fines on all charges, the fines on the counts charging violation of the Insecticide Act of 1910 being $130.

M. L. WILSON, *Acting Secretary of Agriculture.*

1401. Misbranding of Key-Rite General Disinfectant. U. S. v. Interstate Chemical Manufacturing Co. Plea of guilty. Fine, $50. (I. & F. no. 1769. Sample nos. 67295–A, 69862–A.)

This case was based on an interstate shipment of a product which was misbranded because of unwarranted claims appearing in the labeling regarding its alleged effectiveness as an insecticide and disinfectant.

On February 5, 1935, the United States attorney for the District of New Jersey, acting upon a report by the Secretary of Agriculture, filed in the district court an information against the Interstate Chemical Manufacturing Co., a corporation, Jersey City, N. J., alleging shipment by said company on or about January 16, 1934, from the State of New Jersey into the State of New York, of a quantity of Key-Rite General Disinfectant which was a misbranded insecticide and fungicide within the meaning of the Insecticide Act of 1910.

The article was alleged to be misbranded in that the following statements borne on the can label, "Horses Ordinary Mange * * * Hogs * * * Ordinary Mange * * * Dogs * * * Ordinary Mange" and "Disinfectant * * * Closets, drains. As an aid in disinfecting * * * Garbage cans. Wash with mixture of one part Disinfectant to 100 parts water * * * Every home, school, hotel, restaurant, hospital and public place should be scrubbed with a small quantity of Disinfectant in the water", were false and misleading, and by reason of the said statements the article was labeled so as to deceive and mislead the purchaser in that they represented that the article when used as directed would act as an effective insecticide for all varieties of mange, indicated by the term "Ordinary Mange", and when used as directed would disinfect drains, and would act as an effective disinfectant for garbage cans, when used in the proportion of one part of the article to 100 parts of water, and when used in a small quantity in the scrubbing water, would disinfect homes, schools, hotels, restaurants, hospitals, and public places; whereas the article when used as directed would not act as an effective insecticide for all varieties of mange indicated by the term "Ordinary Mange", would not disinfect drains, it was not an effective disinfectant for garbage cans, and would not disinfect homes, schools, hotels, restaurants, hospitals, and public places, when used in the dilution and proportion indicated.

The information also charged a violation of the Food and Drugs Act reported in notice of judgment no. 24544, published under that act.

On February 15, 1935, a plea of guilty was entered on behalf of the defendant company and the court imposed a fine of $50 which covered both violations.

M. L. WILSON, *Acting Secretary of Agriculture.*

1402. Adulteration and misbranding of Purina Flea Powder. U. S. v. Ralston Purina Co. Plea of guilty. Fine, $400 and costs. (I. & F. no. 1771. Sample nos. 46736–A, 65889–A.)

This case was based on interstate shipments of an insecticide which was adulterated and misbranded, since it contained no derris, one of the ingredients declared on the label. The article was further misbranded since it contained inert ingredients in excess of the amount declared.

On April 22, 1935, the United States attorney for the Eastern District of Missouri, acting upon a report by the Secretary of Agriculture, filed in the district court an information against the Ralston Purina Co., a corporation,

St. Louis, Mo., alleging shipment by said company on or about January 26, 1934, from the State of Missouri into the State of Texas, and or about April 11, 1934, from the State of Missouri into the State of Arkansas, of quantities of Purina Flea Powder, which was an adulterated and misbranded insecticide, other than Paris green and lead arsenate, within the meaning of the Insecticide Act of 1910.

The article was alleged to be adulterated in that the statements, "Derris 10% * * * Inert Ingredients 23.5%", borne on the can label, represented that its standard and quality were such that it contained not less than 10 percent of derris and not more than 23.5 percent of inert ingredients; whereas the strength and purity of the article fell below the professed standard and quality under which it was sold, since it contained no derris and did contain inert ingredients in a proportion much greater than 23.5 percent. Adulteration was alleged for the further reason that the article was represented to contain 10 percent of derris, whereas other substances had been substituted for derris.

Misbranding was alleged for the reason that the statements, "Derris 10% * * * Inert Ingredients 23.5%", were false and misleading, and by reason of the said statements the article was labeled so as to deceive and mislead the purchaser, since it contained no derris and did contain inert ingredients in a proportion much greater than 23.5 percent.

On April 29, 1935, a plea of guilty was entered on behalf of the defendant company and the court imposed a fine of $400 and costs.

M. L. WILSON, *Acting Secretary of Agriculture.*

1403. Adulteration and misbranding of B. P. A. Bean Dust. U. S. v. Bridgeville Packing Association. Plea of guilty. Fine, $100. (I. & F. no. 1772. Sample nos. 74654–A, 74655–A.)

This case involved interstate shipments of an insecticide and fungicide which contained smaller proportions of calcium arsenate, monohydrated copper sulphate, and total arsenic as metallic, and a larger proportion of inert ingredients than declared on the label.

On March 13, 1935, the United States attorney for the District of Delaware, acting upon a report by the Secretary of Agriculture, filed in the district court an information against the Bridgeville Packing Association, a corporation, Bridgeville, Del., alleging shipment by said company on or about June 7 and June 15, 1934, from the State of Delaware into the State of Maryland of quantities of B. P. A. Bean Dust which was an adulterated and misbranded insecticide and fungicide within the meaning of the Insecticide Act of 1910. The two shipments of the article were labeled: "B. P. A. 'A' Brand Bean Dust," and "B. P. A. 'B' Brand Bean Dust", respectively.

The information charged adulteration of both brands of the article in that the following statements on the labels, "Calcium Arsenate 19.5% Copper Metallic (Monohydrated Copper Sulphate) 19.5%. Inert Ingredients 61.0%. Total Arsenic as metallic 7.34%", with respect to the "A" brand; and "Calcium Arsenate 9.5% Copper Metallic (Monohydrated Copper Sulphate) 14.5% Inert Ingredients 76.0% Total Arsenic as metallic 4.57%", with respect to the "B" brand, represented that the standard and quality of the article were as set forth in the said statements, whereas the strength and purity of the article fell below the professed standard and quality under which it was sold, since the "A" brand contained calcium arsenate in a proportion less than 19.5 percent; it contained monohydrated copper sulphate in a proportion less than 19.5 percent; it contained total arsenic as metallic in a proportion less than 7.34 percent, and it contained inert ingredients in a proportion greater than 61.0 percent; and the "B" brand contained calcium arsenate in a proportion less than 9.5 percent; it contained monohydrated copper sulphate in a proportion less than 14.5 percent; it contained total arsenic as metallic in a proportion less than 4.57 percent; and it contained inert ingredients in a proportion greater than 76 percent.

Misbranding was alleged for the reason that the above-quoted statements borne on the tags attached to the drums containing the article, were false and misleading, and by reason of the said statements the article was labeled so as to deceive and mislead the purchaser, since it contained smaller proportions of calcium arsenate, monohydrated copper sulphate, and total arsenic as metallic, and contained larger proportions of inert ingredients than so declared.

On March 15, 1935, a plea of guilty was entered on behalf of the defendant company and the court imposed a fine of $100.

M. L. WILSON, *Acting Secretary of Agriculture.*

1404. Misbranding of Bamberger's Antiseptic Bird Wash. U. S. v. Hartz Mountain Products Co. Plea of guilty. Fine, $150. (I. & F. no. 1776. Sample no. 16778–B.)

This case involved a product which was misbranded because of unwarranted claims regarding its alleged effectiveness as an antiseptic, and as a control for certain insects. The labeling was further objectionable, since it failed to declare the inert ingredients present in the article.

On April 5, 1935, the United States attorney for the Southern District of New York, acting upon a report by the Secretary of Agriculture, filed in the district court an information against the Hartz Mountain Products Co., a corporation, New York, N. Y., alleging shipment by said company on or about October 16, 1934, from the State of New York into the State of New Jersey of a quantity of Bamberger's Antiseptic Bird Wash, which was a misbranded insecticide and fungicide within the meaning of the Insecticide Act of 1910.

The article was alleged to be misbranded in that the statements, "Antiseptic", and "For mites, lice, * * * Directions Add one teaspoonful to the bird's bath, or if spraying, add one teaspoonful to each four ounces of water", borne on the bottle label, were false and misleading, and by reason of the said statements the article was labeled so as to deceive and mislead the purchaser, since the article, when used according to directions on the label, would not act as an antiseptic, and when used as directed would not act as an effective insecticide against mites and lice on cage birds. Misbranding was alleged for the further reason that the article consisted partially of an inert substance, namely, water, which substance does not prevent, destroy, repel, or mitigate insects or fungi, and the name and percentage amount of the said inert ingredient were not stated plainly and correctly, or at all, on the bottle label; nor, in lieu thereof, were the name and percentage amount of each ingredient of the article having insecticidal or fungicidal properties, and the total percentage of the inert substances present therein stated plainly and correctly on the label.

On April 12, 1935, a plea of guilty was entered on behalf of the defendant company, and the court imposed a fine of $150.

M. L. WILSON, *Acting Secretary of Agriculture.*

1405. Adulteration and misbranding of Mothgard Camphor Pocket. U. S. v. Louis Weisenfeld, Kermit Kase and Nathan Kase (Gold Star Novelty Co.). Pleas of guilty. Fines, $40. (I. & F. no. 1777. Sample no. 69811–A.)

This case involved a product which was labeled to convey the impression that it contained camphor and would afford protection against moth larvae. Examination showed that it contained no camphor and would not afford the moth protection claimed.

On July 24, 1935, the United States attorney for the Southern District of New York, acting upon a report by the Secretary of Agriculture, filed in the district court an information against Louis Weisenfeld, Kermit Kase, and Nathan Kase, copartners, trading as the Gold Star Novelty Co., New York, N. Y., alleging shipment by said defendants on or about March 29, 1934, from the State of New York into the State of New Jersey of a quantity of a product, known as "Mothgard Camphor Pocket", which was an adulterated and misbranded insecticide within the meaning of the Insecticide Act of 1910.

The article was alleged to be adulterated in that the statement, "Camphor Pocket * * * Camphor fumes will kill all moth larvae", borne on the label, represented that the article consisted in part of camphor; whereas it did not consist in part of camphor, but another substance, namely, naphthalene, had been substituted for camphor.

Misbranding was alleged for the reason that the statements, "Camphor Pocket * * * Camphor fumes will kill all moth larvae", "Mothgard Camphor Pocket Hang in closet—wardrobe bags. Place in drawers—chests—trunks. Camphor fumes will kill all moth larvae", borne on the label, were false and misleading, and by reason of the said statements the article was labeled so as to deceive and mislead the purchaser, since they represented that the article consisted partially of camphor, and when used as directed would kill all moth larvae under all conditions; whereas the article contained no camphor and when used as directed would not kill all moth larvae under all conditions.

On September 23, 1935, the defendants entered pleas of guilty and the court imposed fines totaling $40.

M. L. WILSON, *Acting Secretary of Agriculture.*

1406. Misbranding of McClellan's Orthosol and McClellan's Sheep Dip. U. S. v. McClellan Products, Ltd. Plea of nolo contendere. Defendant placed on probation for two years. (I. & F. no. 1778. Sample nos. 60380–A, 60381–A.)

This case was based on interstate shipments of Orthosol and Sheep Dip which were misbranded, the labeling of the former containing unwarranted claims regarding its alleged disinfecting and sterilizing properties, and the labeling of the latter containing unwarranted insecticidal claims.

On May 15, 1935, the United States attorney for the Southern District of California, acting upon a report by the Secretary of Agriculture, filed in the district court an information against the McClellan Products, Ltd., a corporation, Los Angeles, Calif., alleging shipment by said company in violation of the Insecticide Act of 1910, from the State of California into the State of Oregon, on or about February 16, 1934, of a quantity of McClellan's Orthosol which was a misbranded fungicide, and on or about March 3, 1934, of a quantity of McClellan's Sheep Dip which was a misbranded insecticide and fungicide.

The Orthosol was alleged to be misbranded in that the following statements borne on the can label, "For general disinfection use half a pint of Orthosol to 5 gallons of water. This can be used with a mop, brush or sprayer. * * * For use in Hospitals, Sanitariums and Homes * * * and to sterilize surgical instruments, use a 1 to 2% solution of McClellan's Orthosol Disinfectant", were false and misleading, and by reason of the said statements the article was labeled so as to deceive and mislead the purchaser, since they represented that the article would act as an effective disinfectant for general disinfection when used at the dilution of one-half pint to 5 gallons of water, and that it would sterilize surgical instruments when used in a 1 to 2 percent solution, whereas it would not act as an effective disinfectant for general disinfection when used at the dilution of one-half pint to 5 gallons of water, and it would not sterilize surgical instruments when used at a 1 to 2 percent solution. Misbranding of the Sheep Dip was alleged for the reason that the statements, "Dip For Dogs—Use dilution of 1 part of McClellan's Dip to 80 parts of warm water and wash dog thoroughly, taking special care to remove all scabs and crusts and then saturate affected parts. Repeat as often as necessary", borne on the label, were false and misleading, and by reason of the said statements the article was labeled so as to deceive and mislead the purchaser, since they represented that the article when used as directed would act as an effective treatment for all parasites of the skin of dogs; whereas it would not act as an effective treatment for all parasites of the skin of dogs when used as directed.

The information also charged a violation of the Food and Drugs Act, reported in notices of judgment, published under that act.

On September 18, 1935, the defendant entered a plea of nolo contendere and was placed on probation for two years with the usual conditions.

M. L. WILSON, *Acting Secretary of Agriculture.*

1407. Misbranding of Puritol. U. S. v. Chas. Crompton & Sons, Inc. Plea of nolo contendere. Fine, $5. (I. & F. no. 1779. Sample no. 14540–B.)

This case was based on an interstate shipment of Puritol, an insecticide and fungicide, the labeling of which contained false and misleading claims regarding its alleged effectiveness as a disinfectant and germicide, as a control for mange and certain insects, and as an agency for purifying the air. The label was further objectionable since the article was represented to be nonpoisonous, whereas it contained poisonous ingredients; and since it contained inert substances that were not declared.

On May 15, 1935, the United States attorney for the District of Massachusetts, acting upon a report by the Secretary of Agriculture, filed in the district court an information against Chas. Crompton & Sons, Inc., Lynn, Mass., alleging shipment by said company on or about August 6, 1934, from the State of Massachusetts into the State of New Hampshire of a quantity of Puritol which was a misbranded insecticide and fungicide within the meaning of the Insecticide Act of 1910.

The article was alleged to be misbranded in that the following statements, (bottle and carton) "Contains no poisonous or corrosive ingredients", (circular) "To keep pure air in Hospitals, Houses, School Rooms, Larders, Kitchens, etc., sprinkle freely, and destroy all disease germs, one teaspoonful to one quart of water. For Typhoid, Cholera, Diphtheria, Small Pox, Scarlet Fever, and all Malignant Diseases, the solution should be sprinkled freely in the sick chamber, sinks, closets, urinals, vessels, etc., four teaspoonfuls to one quart of water. * * * For all washing purposes, Scrubbing Floors, House Cleaning, etc., better than soap, one tablespoonful to pail of water. * * * 1 part in 50 of water. Mop stables daily with same solution and keep animals free from infection.", "For horses, to prevent or cure mange, saturate the coat of animal with solution, 1 part in 50 of water", "For lice in chickens, sprinkle floors and nests of henneries, and wash roosts with solution of 1 part in 50 of water", "To destroy all parasites, insects, * * * wash animals (especially neck and head) with 1 part in 50 of water", "* * * keep off flies, etc., wash animals (especially neck and head) with 1 part in 50 of water", "For water bugs, roaches, etc., pour a few drops of the clear, pure disinfectant into the places where the vermin are and they will disappear", appearing in the labeling were false and misleading and by reason of the said statements, the article was labeled so as to deceive and mislead the purchaser, since it contained poisonous ingredients, namely, phenols and coal-tar oils. The article when used as directed would not keep the air in hospitals, houses, school rooms, larders, kitchens, etc., pure, would not destroy all disease germs, and would not act as an effective disinfectant; it would not act as an effective preventive or cure for all varieties of mange on horses, nor would it be effective in the prevention or treatment of any specific variety of mange without repeated treatments; it would not act as an effective insecticide against chicken lice; would not destroy all parasites or all insects that infest animals; nor would it destroy any specific parasite or insect without repeated treatment; it would not keep all species of files off animals, and would not cause water bugs, roaches, or all insects that might be included under the abbreviation "etc.", to disappear. Misbranding was alleged for the further reason that the article consisted partially of inert substances, namely, substances that do not prevent, destroy, repel, or mitigate insects or fungi, and the name and percentage amount of each of the inert ingredients so present therein, were not stated plainly or correctly on the label affixed to the bottle containing the article; nor, in lieu thereof, were the name and percentage amount of each substance or ingredient of the article having insecticidal or fungicidal properties, and the total percentage of the inert substances present, stated plainly and correctly on the said label.

On June 10, 1935, a plea of nolo contendere was entered on behalf of the defendant company and the court imposed a fine of $5.

M. L. WILSON, *Acting Secretary of Agriculture.*

1408. Misbranding of Reade's Antiseptic Animal Soap. U. S. v. Reade Manufacturing Co., Inc. Plea of guilty. Fine, $50. (I. & F. no. 1793. Sample no. 16780–B.)

This case involved a product intended for use as an insecticide and fungicide, the labeling of which contained false and misleading claims regarding its alleged effectiveness as an antiseptic and fungicide, and as a control for certain insects.

On June 17, 1935, the United States attorney for the District of New Jersey, acting upon a report by the Secretary of Agriculture, filed in the district court an information against the Reade Manufacturing Co., Inc., Jersey City, N. J., alleging shipment by said company on or about October 16, 1934, from the State of New Jersey into the State of New York of a quantity of Reade's Antiseptic Animal Soap, which was a misbranded insecticide and fungicide within the meaning of the Insecticide Act of 1910.

The article was alleged to be misbranded in that the statements, "Reade's Antiseptic Animal Soap * * * The antiseptic and germicidal properties of this soap * * * Used regularly, this soap keeps the skin and coat * * * free from vermin * * * The antiseptic and germicidal properties of this soap are helpful in preventing skin troubles such as mange". borne on the can label, were false and misleading, and by reason of the said statements the article was labeled so as to deceive and mislead the purchaser, since they represented that the article when used as directed would act as an antiseptic and germicide, would act as an effective insecticide against all vermin, and would be helpful in preventing skin troubles such as mange; whereas it would not act as an antiseptic or a germicide, would not act as an effective insecticide against all vermin, and would not be helpful in preventing skin troubles, such as mange, when used as directed.

The information also charged a violation of the Food and Drugs Act, reported in notices of judgment published under that act.

On September 17, 1935, a plea of guilty was entered on behalf of the de_ fendant company and the court imposed fines for violations of both acts, the fine on the count charging violation of the Insecticide Act being $50.

M. L. WILSON, *Acting Secretary of Agriculture.*

1409. Adulteration and misbranding of Kleenup Flowable Oil Emulsion. U. S. v. 80 Drums of Kleenup Flowable Oil Emulsion. Default decree of destruction. (I. & F. no. 1780. Sample no. 11934–B.)

This case involved an insecticide which contained ingredients which would be injurious to certain vegetation when used as directed on the label. The labeling bore unwarranted claims regarding the effectiveness of the article in the control of certain insects.

On February 19, 1935, the United States attorney for the District of Utah, acting upon a report by the Secretary of Agriculture, filed in the district court a libel praying seizure and condemnation of 80 drums of Kleenup Flowable Oil Emulsion at Provo, Utah, alleging that the article had been shipped in interstate commerce on or about May 1, 1934, by the California Spray-Chemical Corporation, from Richmond, Calif., and charging adulteration and misbrand. ing in violation of the Insecticide Act of 1910.

The article was alleged to be adulterated in that it contained a substance, or substances, injurious to vegetation when used as directed.

Misbranding was alleged for the reason that the following statements, "Kleenup Flowable Oil Emulsion Orchard Pests For San Jose Scale, European Red Mite and Brown Mite Eggs, Buffalo Three Hopper Eggs, Blister Mite Rust, Mite and Hatching Aphis, Eggs, etc., Use Four Gallons Kleenup to make One Hundred Gallons of Spray", "For Oyster Shell Scale, Leaf Roller Lecanium Scale, Cottony Maple Scale, Elm Tree Scale Use Five to Seven Gallons of Kleenup to make One Hundred Gallons of Spray", "For Peach Twig Borer Use Three to Four Gallons of Kleenup and Three Pounds of Lead Arsenate to make One Hundred Gallons of Spray", "Park Shade Tree and Nursery Insects for scale insects, European Red Mite, etc., Use Four to Five Gallons of Kleenup to make One Hundred Gallons of Spray", borne on the label, were false and misleading and tended to deceive and mislead the purchaser, since the article when used as directed would not be effective against the above-named insects.

On May 3, 1935, no claimant having appeared, judgment of condemnation was entered and it was ordered that the product be destroyed.

M. L. WILSON, *Acting Secretary of Agriculture.*

1410. Adulteration and misbranding of GO–4 and misbranding of G & O Moth Deodorant. U. S. v. Goulard & Olena, Inc. Plea of guilty. Fine, $300. (I. & F. no. 1783. Sample nos. 60917–A, 69827–A, 2163–B.)

This case covered two shipments of GO–4, an insecticide and fungicide, and one shipment of G & O Moth Deodorant, an insecticide. Examination showed that the GO–4 would cause injury to certain vegetation when used as directed; that one lot of the GO–4 contained a smaller proportion of nicotine sulphate and a larger proportion of water-soluble arsenic as metallic than declared; and that the G & O Moth Deodorant would not afford the moth protection claimed.

On May 15, 1935, the United States attorney for the District of New Jersey, acting upon a report by the Secretary of Agriculture, filed in the district court an information against Goulard & Olena, Inc., trading at Jersey City, N. J., alleging shipment by said company in violation of the Insecticide Act of 1910, on or about March 15, 1934, from the State of New Jersey into the State of Illinois, of a quantity of G & O Moth Deodorant which was misbranded, and on or about April 5 and April 19, 1934, from the State of New Jersey into the States of Indiana and Connecticut, respectively, of quantities of GO–4, which was adulterated and misbranded.

The information charged that a portion of the GO–4 was adulterated in that the statements, "Nicotine Sulphate 5.00% * * * Water Soluble Arsenic as Metallic not over .50%", borne on the labels, represented that the article contained not less than 5 percent of nicotine sulphate and not more than 0.5 percent of water-soluble arsenic as metallic; whereas its strength and purity fell below the professed standard and quality under which it was sold, since it contained less than 5 percent of nicotine sulphate and more than 0.5 percent of water-soluble arsenic as metallic. Adulteration was alleged with respect to both lots of the GO–4 for the reason that it contained a substance, or substances, injurious to vegetation when used as directed.

Misbranding was alleged with respect to a portion of the GO–4 for the reason that the statements, "Nicotine Sulphate 5.00% * * * Water Soluble Arsenic as Metallic not over .50%", "GO–4 These Bugs and Diseases Before They Go For Your Garden! * * * Safe * * * For certain Kinds of Bugs—Aphis—Plant Disease on Fruits–Shrubs–Vegetables–Flowers–Trees", "How and when to use GO–4 * * * Apples: * * * Grapes: * * *' Beans. * * * Flowers, Shrubs, potted Plants, etc.", appearing in the labeling, were false and misleading, and for the further reason that the article was labeled so as to deceive and mislead the purchaser in that the said statements represented that the article contained not less than 5 percent of nicotine sulphate and not more than 0.5 percent of water-soluble arsenic as metallic, and could be safely used on all plants and on the vegetation :designated; whereas it contained less than 5 percent of nicotine sulphate and more than 0.5 percent of water-soluble arsenic as metallic; it could not be safely used on all plants and on the designated vegetation, but would cause serious injury to certain plants, and cause serious injury to apples, grapes, and beans and to certain flowers, shrubs, and potted plants. Misbranding of the remainder of the GO–4 was alleged for the reason that the statements, "Apples * * * 1st Spraying—Apply before blossoms open, one (1) lb. to 12½ gallons of water. 2nd Spraying—Same dose just as blossoms fall, directing the spray into the calyx cup. 3rd Spraying—Same dose three weeks later", borne on the label, were false and misleading and by reason of the said statements the article was labeled so as to deceive and mislead the purchaser, since they represented that the article could be safely used on apples; whereas it could not be safely so used on apples, but such use would cause serious injury thereto.

Misbranding of the G & O Moth Deodorant was alleged for the reason that the statement, "The contents of this package will kill moths in 20 cubic feet of tightly enclosed space", borne on the label, was false and misleading; and by reason of the said statement the article was labeled so as to deceive and mislead the purchaser in that it represented that the article when used as directed would kill moths, whereas the article when used as directed would not kill moths.

On May 24, 1935, a plea of guilty was entered on behalf of the defendant company and the court imposed a fine of $300.

M. L. WILSON, *Acting Secretary of Agriculture.*

1411. Adulteration and misbranding of Moca Calcium Arsenate. U. S. v. 9 Drums of Moca Calcium Arsenate. Product released under bond to be relabeled. (I. & F. no. 1784. Sample no. 26120–B.)

This case involved a shipment of Moca Calcium Arsenate which was adulterated and misbranded because of the presence of calcium compounds other than calcium arsenate, and siliceous material of the nature of talc. The article was further misbranded because it was a product other than Paris green or lead arsenate, containing arsenic, and did not have the total amount of arsenic and the amount of arsenic in water-soluble form expressed as percentum of metallic arsenic declared on the label, and failed to bear on the label a statement indicating the active and inert ingredients.

On March 8, 1935, the United States attorney for the District of Utah, acting upon a report by the Secretary of Agriculture, filed in the district court a libel praying seizure and condemnation of nine drums of Moca Calcium Arsenate at Ogden, Utah, alleging that the article had been shipped in interstate commerce on or about March 9, 1934, by the California Spray-Chemical Corporation, from Richmond, Calif., and charging adulteration and misbranding in violation of the Insecticide Act of 1910.

The article was alleged to be adulterated in that siliceous material and other calcium compounds had been substituted in part for calcium arsenate.

Misbranding was alleged for the reason that the statement "Calcium Arsenate" was false and misleading and tended to deceive and mislead the purchaser. Misbranding was alleged for the further reason that the article was a product other than Paris green or lead arsenate containing arsenic, and the total amount of arsenic expressed as percentage of metallic arsenic was not stated on the label; it contained arsenic in water-soluble form, and did not have the amount thereof expressed as percentage of metallic arsenic on the label; it consisted partially of inert substances, that is, substances other than calcium arsenate, and did not have the. name and percentage amount of each inert ingredient plainly and correctly stated on the label, nor did the label bear a statement of the name and percentage amount of the ingredient having insecticidal properties, and the total percentage of inert ingredients.

On May 22, 1935, the California Spray Chemical Corporation, having appeared as claimant and having admitted that the product was not properly labeled, judgment was entered ordering that it be released to the claimant under bond conditioned that it be relabeled under the supervision of this Department.

M. L. WILSON, *Acting Secretary of Agriculture.*

1412. Adulteration and misbranding of powdered arsenate of calcium. U. S. v. 500 Bags of Powdered Arsenate of Calcium. Default decree of condemnation and destruction. (I. & F. no. 1785. Sample no. 66501–A.)

This case involved a shipment of powdered arsenate of calcium which contained water-soluble arsenic, expressed as arsenic pentoxide, materially in excess of the amount declared on the label, and in sufficient amount to render the product injurious to certain vegetation on which its use was recommended.

On March 15, 1935, the United States attorney for the Southern District of Mississippi, acting upon a report by the Secretary of Agriculture, filed in the district court a libel praying seizure and condemnation of 500 bags of Orchard Brand Powdered Arsenate of Calcium at Meridian, Miss., alleging that the article had been shipped in interstate commerce on or about May 18, 1934, by the General Chemical Co., from East St. Louis, Ill., and charging adulteration and misbranding in violation of the Insecticide Act of 1910.

The article was alleged to be adulterated in that its strength and purity fell below the professed standard and quality under which it was sold, and for the further reason that it contained substances injurious to vegetation when used as directed.

Misbranding was alleged for the reason that the statements, "Arsenic in Water Soluble form not more than 0.75 per cent. Arsenic Pentoxide Equivalent to Metallic Arsenic 0.49 per cent.", and "We Guarantee that the Contents of this Package when Shipped by us Complied with the Statement of Composition Contained Hereon", borne on the label, were false and misleading and tended to deceive and mislead the purchasers, since it contained more water-soluble arsenic pentoxide and more water-soluble arsenic expressed as metallic arsenic than claimed. Misbranding was alleged for the further reason that the statement, "For Liquid Application on * * * Shade Trees One and One Half to Two and One Half Lbs.", on the labels, represented that the article could be safely used on shade trees; whereas it would seriously injure many shade trees when used as directed.

On October 2, 1935, no claimant having appeared, judgment of condemnation was entered and it was ordered that the product be destroyed.

M. L. WILSON, *Acting Secretary of Agriculture.*

1413. Misbranding of Aid–All Flea–Rid and Insecticide Spray. U. S. v. The Aid–All Co., Inc. Plea of guilty. Fine, $150. (I. & F. no. 1786. Sample nos. 68348–A, 71730–A.)

This case was based on interstate shipments of insecticides which were misbranded because of unwarranted claims in the labeling regarding their alleged effectiveness in the control of certain insects. The product Aid-All Flea-Rid was further misbranded because of failure to declare the inert ingredients present.

On April 20, 1935, the United States attorney for the District of New Jersey, acting upon a report by the Secretary of Agriculture, filed in the district court an information against the Aid-All Co., Inc., Newark, N. J., alleging shipment by said company on or about March 30 and May 4, 1934, from the State of New Jersey into the State of Massachusetts of quantities of Aid-All Flea-Rid and Insecticide Spray, which were misbranded insecticides within the meaning of the Insecticide Act of 1910.

The information charged that the Aid-All Flea-Rid was misbranded in that the following statements, "Aid-All Flea-Rid An Excellent Remedy to Rid Dogs of Fleas and Vermin Directions Add one tablespoonful of Flea-Rid to one pint of water. Sponge dog freely and allow it to dry", borne on the bottle label, were false and misleading, and by reason of the said statements the article was labeled so as to deceive and mislead the purchaser, since the article when used as directed would not rid dogs of fleas and all vermin. Misbranding of the Flea-Rid was alleged for the further reason that it consisted partially of inert ingredients, namely, water and alcohol, substances that do not prevent, destroy, repel, or mitigate insects, and the percentage amount of each of the inert ingredients so present in the article was not stated plainly and correctly on the label affixed to each of the bottles containing the article; nor, in lieu thereof, were the names and percentage amounts of each ingredient of the article having insecticidal properties, and the total percentage of the inert substances present stated plainly and correctly on the label.

Misbranding of the Insecticide Spray was alleged for the reason that the statements, "Fleas Etc.—mix with equal parts of water as a spray Roaches, Ants Etc.—use undiluted", borne on the bottle label, were false and misleading, and by reason of the said statement the article was labeled so as to deceive and mislead the purchaser, since they represented that the article when used as directed would act as an effective insecticide against fleas and all insects that might be included under the abbreviation "Etc.", whereas the article, when used as directed, would not act as an effective insecticide against fleas, nor would it act as an effective insecticide against all insects that might be included under the abbreviation "Etc."

On May 7, 1935, a plea of guilty was entered on behalf of the defendant company, and the court imposed a fine of $150.

M. L. WILSON, *Acting Secretary of Agriculture.*

1414. Misbranding of Rotecide Insect Dust.   U. S. v. Rotenone Products Co.. Inc. Plea of guilty.   Fine, $40.   (I. & F. no. 1790. Sample nos. 49902–A, 7352–B.)

This case was based on shipments of an insecticide the labeling of which contained unwarranted claims regarding its effectiveness in the control of insects. The labeling was further objectionable, since the product was represented to be nonpoisonous, whereas it was poisonous, and since the inert ingredients present were not declared.

On May 15, 1935, the United States attorney for the District of New Jersey, acting upon a report by the Secretary of Agriculture, filed in the district court an information against the Rotenone Products Co., Inc., East Orange, N. J., alleging shipment by said company on or about August 22, 1933, and March 8. 1934, from the State of New Jersey into the State of New York of quantities of Rotecide Insect Dust which was a misbranded insecticide within the meaning of the Insecticide Act of. 1910.

The article was alleged to be misbranded in that the following statements, "Rotecide Insect Dust * * * A Superfine Product For The Farmer, Greenhouseman, Gardener, Stable, Dairy Barn, Dog Kennel, Poultry House, and for Domestic Vermin * * * Rotecide Dust effectively controls: * * * Cut Worms, Caterpillars * * * Domestic Vermin", "Non-Poisonous To Man, Animal or Bird", "Rotecide Dust effectively controls * * * Domestic Vermin And various other insects", "Rotecide Insect Dust is absolute protection against insect infestations usually common in Stables, Kennels, Barns and Poultry Houses. Also, against * * * other Domestic Insects", "Fruits and Vegetables dusted with Rotecide Insect Dust are protected from insects", "Directions For Plants Dust thoroughly, covering all surfaces with a light layer of dust. Be sure to well cover the new growth. The use of Rotecide Dust cannot begin too early as no plant is too young to be protected. Dust after watering or after dew has begun to fall in the early morn or late afternoon. Applications should be re-applied after rains. For small areas use a hand duster. For Animals and Fowl Dust into the dry hair of the animal or rub dust upon head and under wings of fowl. A generous application will do no harm. For Stable, Kennel and Home Sprinkle Dust into all corners, crevices and places where insects usually habitate. After all insects disappear give one extra application to prevent reinfestation", borne on the package label, were false and misleading, and by reason of the said statements the article was labeled so as to deceive and mislead the purchaser, since the article was not nonpoisonous to man or to animals or to birds, but would be poisonous, and the said article when used as directed, would not act as an effective control for cut worms, caterpillars and all domestic vermin; it would not act as an effective control for all vermin and all insects that infest animals; it would not furnish absolute protection against insect infestations usually common in stables, kennels, barns, and poultry houses, and against all other domestic insects; it would not protect fruits and vegetables from all insects; and it would not act as an effective insecticide against all insects that infest or attack plants, animals, fowls, stables, kennels, and homes. Misbranding was alleged for the further reason that the article consisted partially of inert substances, namely, substances other than derris resins, which substances do not prevent, destroy, repel, or mitigate insects, and the name and percentage amount of each inert substance or ingredient present in the article were not stated plainly and correctly on the label; nor, in lieu thereof, were the name and percentage amount of each ingredient of the article having insecticidal properties, and the total percentage of the inert substances present stated plainly and correctly on the label.

On May 24, 1935, a plea of guilty was entered on behalf of the defendant company, and the court imposed a fine of $40.

M. L. WILSON, *Acting Secretary of Agriculture.*

1415. Adulteration and misbranding of chlorinated lime. U. S. v. 420 Cans of Chlorinated Lime. Default decree of condemnation and destruction. (I. & F. no. 1796. Sample no. 28996–B.)

This case involved a product which contained a smaller proportion of available chlorine and a larger proportion of inert ingredients than declared on the label.

On April 15, 1935, the United States attorney for the District of Massachusetts, acting upon a report by the Secretary of Agriculture, filed in the district court a libel praying seizure and condemnation of 420 cans of chlorinated lime at Boston, Mass., alleging that the article had been shipped in interstate commerce on or about March 27, 1935, by the Sunlight Chemical Corporation, from Phillipsdale, R. I., and charging adulteration and misbranding in violation of the Insecticide Act of 1910.

The article was alleged to be adulterated in that its standard and quality were represented to be such that it contained available chlorine not less than 30 percent and inert ingredients not more than 70 percent, whereas it fell below such standard.

Misbranding was alleged for the reason that the statements, "Available Chlorine not less than 30 percent. Inert Ingredients not more than 70 percent", borne on the can label, were false and misleading and tended to deceive and mislead the purchaser.

On May 27, 1955, no claimant having appeared, judgment of condemnation was entered and it was ordered that the product be destroyed.

M. L. WILSON, *Acting Secretary of Agriculture.*

1416. Adulteration and misbranding of Nico Dust No. 110. U. S. v. 2 Drums of Nico Dust No. 110. Default decree of condemnation and destruction. (I. & F. no. 1797. Sample no. 12519–B.)

This case involved an insecticide that contained a smaller proportion of nicotine, the active ingredient, and a larger proportion of inert ingredients than declared on the label.

On April 16, 1935, the United States attorney for the District of Arizona, acting upon a report by the Secretary of Agriculture, filed in the district court a libel praying seizure and condemnation of two drums of Nico Dust No. 110 at Phoenix, Ariz., alleging that the article had been shipped in interstate commerce on or about July 3, 1934, by the Nico Dust Manufacturing Co., from Los Angeles, Calif., and charging adulteration and misbranding in violation of the Insecticide Act of 1910.

The article was alleged to be adulterated in that its strength or purity fell below the professed standard or quality under which it was sold.

Misbranding was alleged for the reason that the statements, "Active ingredients nicotine not less than 2.75% inert ingredients spec. dust composing carrier not more than 97.25%", were false and misleading and tended to deceive and mislead the purchaser, since the article contained 1.66 percent of nicotine and 98.34 percent of inert ingredients.

On May 6, 1935, no claimant having appeared, judgment of condemnation was entered and it was ordered that the product be destroyed.

M. L. WILSON, *Acting Secretary of Agriculture.*

1417. Adulteration and misbranding of C–D–Cide 15 Chlorine Disinfectant. U. S. v. 16 Cartons of C–D–Cide 15 Chlorine Disinfectant. Default decree of condemnation and destruction. (I. & F. no. 1799. Sample no. 31320–B.)

This case involved an interstate shipment of C–D–Cide 15 Chlorine Disinfectant, a fungicide within the meaning of the law. Examination showed that the article contained a smaller proportion of available chlorine and a larger proportion of inert ingredients than declared on the label, and that it was not a concentrated finely powdered chlorine as claimed. The labeling was further objectionable because of unwarranted claims as to the germ-killing and disinfectant properties of the article.

On April 23, 1935, the United States attorney for the District of Oregon, acting upon a report by the Secretary of Agriculture, filed in the district court a libel praying seizure and condemnation of 16 cartons of C-D-Cide 15 Chlorine Disinfectant at Portland, Oreg., alleging that the article had been shipped in interstate commerce on or about September 26, 1934, by the Petaluma Laboratories, from Petaluma, Calif., and charging adulteration and misbranding in violation of the Insecticide Act of 1910.

The article was alleged to be adulterated in that its strength and purity fell below the professed standard and quality under which it was sold, namely: (Carton) "Available Chlorine, over 15% Sodium Chloride and other inert ingredients 85%."

Misbranding was alleged for the reason that the following statements appearing in the labeling, (carton) "Available Chlorine, over 15% Sodium Chloride and other inert ingredients 85% * * * Kills all Germs", (circular) "C-D-Cide '15' is a concentrated finely powdered chlorine * * * because it is very light and fluffy, it goes farther than three pounds of any other 15% chlorine product on the market", "Used as a disinfectant spray, add one teaspoonful to each gallon or one tablespoonful to each three gallons of water", were false and misleading and tended to deceive and mislead the purchaser since the article contained less than 15 percent of available chlorine and more than 85 percent of inert ingredients; it would not kill all germs; it was not a concentrated, finely powdered chlorine; it would not go farther than three pounds of any 15 percent chlorine on the market; and it was not an effective disinfectant in the dilutions specified. The libel also charged a violation of the Food and Drugs Act reported in notice of judgment no. 24550, published under that act.

On June 25, 1935, no claimant having appeared, judgment of condemnation was entered and it was ordered that the product be destroyed.

M. L. WILSON, *Acting Secretary of Agriculture.*

1418. Adulteration and misbranding of B-K Bacili Kil. U. S. v. 33 Bottles of B-K Bacili Kil. Default decree of condemnation and destruction. (I. & F. no. 1800. Sample no. 11510–B.)

This case involved a fungicide that contained a smaller proportion of the active ingredient, sodium hypochlorite, and a larger proportion of the inert ingredients than declared on the label.

On April 24, 1935, the United States attorney for the Southern District of Texas, acting upon a report by the Secretary of Agriculture, filed in the district court a libel praying seizure and condemnation of 33 bottles of B-K Bacili Kil at Houston, Tex., consigned by the General Laboratories, Inc., alleging that the article had been shipped in interstate commerce on or about November 15, 1933, from Wyandotte, Mich., into the State of Texas, and charging that it was an adulterated and misbranded fungicide within the meaning of the Insecticide Act of 1910.

The article was alleged to be adulterated in that its strength and purity fell below the professed standard and quality under which it was sold.

Misbranding was alleged for the reason that the statements on the carton and bottle labels, "Active ingredient sodium hypochlorite 3.50 per cent Inert ingredients 96.50 per cent", were false and misleading and tended to deceive and mislead purchasers.

On June 29, 1935, no claimant having appeared, judgment of condemnation was entered and it was ordered that the product be destroyed.

M. L. WILSON, *Acting Secretary of Agriculture.*

1419. Adulteration of Orthol K Medium. U. S. v. 18 Drums of Orthol K Medium. Consent decree ordering product released under bond to be reconditioned. (I. & F. no. 1805. Sample no. 31334–B.)

This case involved a product which was intended for use as an insecticide but which would be injurious to vegetation when so used.

On May 6, 1935, the United States attorney for the District of Idaho, acting upon a report by the Secretary of Agriculture, filed in the district court a libel praying seizure and condemnation of 18 drums of Orthol K Medium at New Plymouth, Idaho, alleging that the article had been shipped in interstate commerce on or about May 2, 1934, by the California Spray-Chemical Corporation, from Richmond, Calif., and charging adulteration in violation of the Insecticide Act of 1910.

The article was alleged to be adulterated in that it was an oil emulsion for insecticidal purposes, was completely broken down, and in its present condition would be injurious to vegetation upon which it was intended to be used.

On May 31, 1935, the California Spray-Chemical Corporation, claimant, having consented to the entry of a decree, judgment was entered ordering that the product be released to the claimant under bond conditioned that it be returned to the factory for remixing and that it should not be sold until brought up to the standard requirements for such products.

M. L. WILSON, *Acting Secretary of Agriculture.*

1420. Adulteration and misbranding of E-Z. U. S. v. 21 Cases of E-Z. Default decree of condemnation and destruction. (I. & F. no. 1807. Sample no. 36278-B.)

This case involved a fungicide which was adulterated and misbranded, since it contained a smaller percentage of the active ingredient, sodium hypochlorite, and a larger percentage of inert ingredients than declared on the label. The article was further misbranded because of false and misleading claims in the labeling regarding its strength and alleged harmlessness and sterilizing properties.

On May 28, 1935, the United States attorney for the District of Rhode Island, acting upon a report by the Secretary of Agriculture, filed in the district court a libel praying seizure and condemnation of 21 cases, each containing 12 quart bottles of E-Z, at Newport, R. I., alleging that the article had been shipped in interstate commerce on or about February 16, 1935, by the E-Z Products Co., from New Bedford, Mass., and charging that the article was an adulterated and misbranded fungicide within the meaning of the Insecticide Act of 1910.

The article was alleged to be adulterated in that the statements, "Active Ingredients Sodium Hypochlorite 5% Inert Ingredients 95%", borne on the bottle label, represented that its standard and quality were such that it contained an active ingredient, sodium· hypochlorite, in the proportion of not less than 5 percent, and contained inert ingredients in the proportion of not more than 95 percent; whereas its strength and purity fell below the professed standard and quality under which it was sold, since it contained less than 5 percent of sodium hypochlorite, approximately 2.66 percent of sodium hypochlorite, and it contained more than 95 percent of inert ingredients.

Misbranding was alleged for the reason that the statements, (bottle) "Active Ingredients Sodium Hypochlorite 5% Inert Ingredients 95%", "E-Z is a concentrated sodium hypochlorite", "Its harmlessness * * * are well known to physicians and chemists", "Sterilizer * * * The use of E-Z as a sterilizer", (shipping case) "Sterilizer * * *", appearing in the labeling, were false and misleading, and by reason of the said statements the article was labeled so as to deceive and mislead the purchaser, since they represented that the article contained not less than 5 percent of sodium hypochlorite, and not more than 95 percent of inert ingredients, that it was a concentrated sodium hypochlorite solution, that it was a sterilizer, and that it was harmless; whereas the article contained less than 5 percent of sodium hypochlorite; it contained more than 95 percent of inert ingredients, it was not a concentrated sodium hypochlorite solution, it was not a sterilizer, and it was not harmless, but was poisonous.

On June 24, 1935, no claimant having appeared, judgment of condemnation was entered and it was ordered that the product be destroyed.

M. L. WILSON, *Acting Secretary of Agriculture.*

1421. Adulteration and misbranding of Lucky Solution. U. S. v. 120 Bottles of Lucky Solution. Default decree of condemnation and destruction. (I. & F. no. 1808. Sample no. 28589-B.)

This case involved a product which was adulterated and misbranded, since it contained a smaller proportion of the active ingredient, sodium hypochlorite, and a larger proportion of inert ingredients than declared on the label. The article was further misbranded because of unwarranted claims in the labeling regarding its alleged germicidal, disinfectant, and cleaning properties.

On May 23, 1935, the United States attorney for the Northern District of Ohio, acting upon a report by the Secretary of Agriculture, filed in the district court a libel praying seizure and condemnation of 120 bottles of Lucky Solution at Youngstown, Ohio, alleging that the article had been shipped in interstate commerce on or about November 3, 1934, by the Lucky Chemical Co., Inc., from Pittsburgh, Pa., and charging adulteration and misbranding in violation of the Insecticide Act of 1910.

The article was alleged to be adulterated since it fell below the professed standard and quality under which it was sold, namely, "Active Ingredients Sodium Hypochlorite 5.25% by Wt. Inert Ingredients 94.75% by Wt."

Misbranding was alleged for the reason that the following statements appearing in the labeling were false and misleading and tended to deceive and mislead the purchaser: "Active Ingredients Sodium Hypochlorite 5.25% by Wt. Inert Ingredients 94.75% by Wt. * * * Kills Germs * * * The Sensational New Luck Disinfects and Cleans in One Single Operation * * * To Clean and Sweeten Dental Plates Soak Fifteen Minutes or Overnight in this Solution * * * For Toilet Bowls Add One-half Cup Lucky to Bowl, Stir Well. Add Three Tablespoonfuls Vinegar Let Stand Two Hours or Overnight. Flush Drains with Cupful Pure Lucky Follow with Hot Water in Five Minutes."

On June 19, 1935, no claimant having appeared, judgment of condemnation was entered and it was ordered that the product be destroyed.

M. L. WILSON, *Acting Secretary of Agriculture.*

1422. Misbranding of Calgreen. U. S. v. 1,089 Bags of Calgreen. Default decree of destruction. (I. & F. no. 1811. Sample nos. 22921–B, 23172–B.)

This case involved an insecticide that contained water-soluble arsenic (expressed as metallic arsenic) in excess of the amount declared on the label.

On June 12, 1935, the United States attorney for the District of Minnesota, acting upon a report by the Secretary of Agriculture, filed in the district court a libel praying seizure and condemnation of 1,089 bags of Calgreen at Duluth, Minn., alleging that the article had been shipped in interstate commerce on or about January 22, 1935, by the Chipman Chemical Co., Inc., from Bound Brook, N. J., and charging that the article was a misbranded insecticide within the meaning of the Insecticide Act of 1910.

The article was alleged to be misbranded in that the statement, "Water soluble arsenic (as metallic) not more than 2.0 per cent", was false and misleading and tended to deceive and mislead the purchaser, since it contained more than 2.0 percent of water-soluble arsenic.

On August 21, 1935, no claimant having appeared, judgment was entered ordering that the product be destroyed.

M. L. WILSON, *Acting Secretary of Agriculture.*

1423. Misbranding of Mulsoid Sulfur. U. S. v. 161 Cartons of Mulsoid Sulfur. Consent decree of condemnation. Product released under bond to be relabeled. (I. & F. no. 1815. Sample nos. 35135–B, 35411–B.)

Sample cans of Mulsoid Sulfur taken from the shipment involved in this case were found to contain less than 4 pounds, the weight declared on the label.

On July 5, 1935, the United States attorney for the Southern District of Ohio, acting upon a report by the Secretary of Agriculture, filed in the district court a libel praying seizure and condemnation of 161 cartons of Mulsoid Sulfur at Cincinnati, Ohio, alleging that the article had been shipped in interstate commerce on or about April 11, 1935, by the Sherwin-Williams Co., from Bound Brook, N. J., and charging that it was a misbranded fungicide within the meaning of the Insecticide Act of 1910.

The article was alleged to be misbranded in that the statement "Four Pounds Net Weight", borne on the carton label, was false and misleading and tended to deceive and mislead the purchaser, since the net weight of the product contained in each of the cartons was less than 4 pounds.

On August 29, 1935, the Sherwin-Williams Co., claimant, having admitted the allegations of the libel and having consented to the entry of a decree, judgment of condemnation was entered and it was ordered that the product be released under bond conditioned that it be correctly labeled.

M. L. WILSON, *Acting Secretary of Agriculture.*

1424. Adulteration and misbranding of Mulsoid Sulfur. U. S. v. 111 Packages of Mulsoid Sulfur. Decree of condemnation. Product released under bond to be relabeled. (I. & F. no. 1816. Sample no. 36467–B.)

This case involved a product which contained a smaller proportion of the active ingredient, sulphur, and a larger proportion of the inert ingredients than declared on the label.

On July 10, 1935, the United States attorney for the District of Massachusetts, acting upon a report by the Secretary of Agriculture, filed in the district court a libel praying seizure and condemnation of 111 packages of Mulsoid Sulfur at Boston, Mass., alleging that the article had been shipped in interstate commerce on or about June 10, 1935, by the Sherwin-Williams Co., from Bound Brook, N. J., and charging that it was an adulterated and misbranded insecticide and fungicide within the meaning of the Insecticide Act of 1910.

The article was alleged to be adulterated in that the statements, "Sulfur not less than 95% Inert Ingredients not more than 5%", borne on the packages containing the article, represented that it contained not less than 95 percent of sulphur, and not more than 5 percent of inert ingredients; whereas the product fell below the professed standard and quality under which it was sold, since it contained less than 95 percent of sulphur, and contained more than 5 percent of inert ingredients.

Misbranding was alleged for the reason that the following statements, "Four Pounds Net Weight * * * Active Ingredient-Sulfur, not less than 95% Inert Ingredients Not more than 5%", borne on the packages, were false and misleading, and by reason of the said statements the article was labeled so as to deceive and mislead the purchaser, since it contained less than 95 percent of sulphur, and contained more than 5 percent of inert ingredients.

On August 30, 1935, the Sherwin-Williams Co., Cleveland, Ohio, having appeared as claimant for the property and having admitted the allegations of the libel, judgment of condemnation was entered and it was ordered that the product be released under bond conditioned that it be properly relabeled.

M. L. WILSON, *Acting Secretary of Agriculture.*

1425. Misbranding of Wolf's Gardite. U. S. v. 77 Cases of Wolf's Gardite. Default decree of condemnation and destruction. (I. & F. no. 1822. Sample no. 32313–B.)

This case involved a shipment of Wolf's Gardite which was misbranded because of unwarranted claims in the labeling regarding its alleged effectiveness in the control of certain insects.

On August 6, 1935, the United States attorney for the Southern District of Iowa, acting upon a report by the Secretary of Agriculture, filed in the district court a libel praying seizure and condemnation of 77 cases of Wolf's Gardite at Des Moines, Iowa, alleging that the article had been shipped in interstate commerce on or about June 3, 1934, by the Wolf Chemical Co., from Centralia, Mo., and charging that it was a misbranded insecticide within the meaning of the Insecticide Act of 1910. The article was labeled in part: "Wolf's Gardite made to satisfy—guards gardens—Gardite is excellent for certain bugs and worms on melon, cucumber and pumpkin vines, cabbage, rosebushes, and some other plants and flowers, * * * Gardite may also be used for certain vermin that infest dogs, poultry, horses, cattle, sheep and hogs."

The article was alleged to be misbranded in that the above-quoted statements borne on the package label were false and misleading, and by reason of the said statements the article was labeled so as to deceive and mislead the purchaser, since it would not guard gardens against all bugs and worms on melons, cucumbers, pumpkins, cabbage, rosebushes, and other plants and flowers implied in the phrase "Certain Bugs and Worms", and would not be an effective treatment for certain vermin infesting dogs, poultry, horses, cattle, sheep, and hogs, when used as directed.

On September 23, 1935, no claimant having appeared, judgment of condemnation was entered and it was ordered that the product be destroyed.

M. L. WILSON, *Acting Secretary of Agriculture.*

INDEX TO NOTICES OF JUDGMENT 1376-1425

258

Lightning Source UK Ltd.
Milton Keynes UK
UKHW021852121118
332198UK00006B/348/P

9 780331 386844